WORLD TRADE CENTER

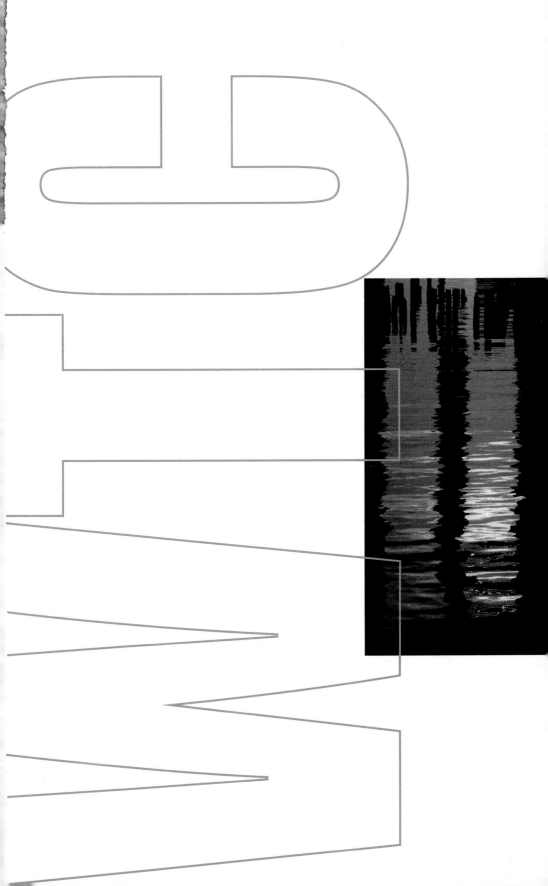

CONTENTS

world tra

1   2   3

TEXTS BY
PETER SKINNER

EDITORIAL PROJECT
VALERIA MANFERTO DE FABIANIS

GRAPHIC DESIGN
PATRIZIA BALOCCO LOVISETTI

WHITE STAR PUBLISHERS

WS White Star Publishers® is a registered
trademark property of Edizioni White Star s.r.l.

© 2002, 2011 Edizioni White Star s.r.l.
Via M. Germano, 10 - 13100 Vercelli, Italy
www.whitestar.it

Revised edition in 2011

ISBN: 978-88-544-0585-1
1 2 3 4 5 6   15 14 13 12 11

Printed in Indonesia

PREFACE

The hijacked planes that zeroed in on New York and Washington with such murderous accuracy obviously chose their targets for a reason. They didn't attack Los Angeles and Miami, after all. Why not? It's reasonable to assume that they chose cities and buildings that they believed had great symbolic and actual potency: the respective headquarters of the military and financial institutions whose decisions have tremendous impact throughout the globe.

As we've seen from the outpouring of support from around the world, millions of people love and admire the United States and its pre-eminent urban centers.

But others hate us passionately. Not, despite what some say, because we are the land of the free and good, but because the nation has embraced policies from which they feel they've suffered. Driven by calculated strategy and suicidal fanaticism, they've dealt a terrific blow to proud towers and command centers alike.

New Yorkers are rolling with the blow magnificently, despite the added shock of having it come both figuratively and literally out of the clear blue sky, shattering our sense of invulnerability. But that sense always rested on a truncated reading of history. While the particular form of the attack was fiendishly novel, New York, over nearly four centuries, has repeatedly been the object of murderous intentions. Through a combination of luck and

12
THE SHATTERED LATTICE THAT SOON
BECAME AN IMAGE RECOGNIZED THE
WORLD OVER.

12-13
AT DUSK, THE WORLD FINANCIAL CENTER
(FOREGROUND) AND THE TWIN TOWERS
TOOK ON A GOLDEN GLOW, REFLECTING
THE SETTING SUN.

power, we have escaped many of the intended blows, but not all of them, and our forebears often feared that worse might yet befall them.

In recent decades, some opponents of the expanding global cultural and economic order of which New York and Washington were seen as headquarters, turned to terror. The resulting mayhem seldom touched New York's shores—the first World Trade Center attack was a notable exception—but fantasies about urban destruction exploded in popular culture. The popularity of cinematic depictions of overseas (or alien) predators wreaking havoc on New York and Washington, with the World Trade Center and Statue of Liberty as attendant casualties, was perhaps also fueled by antagonism to Big Government and Big Corporations.

Now these fantasies have been horribly realized—one reason that we've repeatedly heard stunned witnesses exclaiming the devastation seemed "unreal" or "just like a movie." This is not to say that terrorists are copycats and that Hollywood's to blame, but rather that cultural producers, like almost everyone else, tend to assume that New York and Washington are the likeliest targets.

One consequence of reality having caught up to fiction might be a new reluctance to spin such fantasies—a reissue of "Independence Day" was just postponed—though it's equally likely that someone is already hard at work on a mini-series.

More hopefully, our shattered sense of invulnerability will be replaced by a sober appreciation of the fact that, even as we mourn our casualties, take prudent precautions to prevent similar attacks, help track down and punish those responsible, and reconstruct our city, our generation of New Yorkers, like those that preceded ours, has witnessed and survived a cataclysm even worse than our imaginations had been able to conceive.

14-15
THE VIEW THAT WAS GONE FOREVER:
THE TWIN TOWERS NO LONGER RISE
BEHIND THE WINTER GARDEN, DWARFING
THE WORLD FINANCIAL CENTER TOWERS.
IN THE FOREGROUND: NORTH COVE
HARBOR.

New York! The fabled city with the dramatic skyline, beacon for the best and the brightest, for the fortune seeker, the immigrant—for anyone in search of opportunity. But New York is young and has to create its own myths. New York does this superbly—and believes absolutely in its own grandiose projections. New Yorkers' lives are shaped by images: they are convinced the city offers the newest,

city was booming; the future was bright and beckoning.

Too easily New York forgets past crises—even though their causes and results live on. In retrospect they seem less acute; in fact they are more numerous and serious than New Yorkers want to admit. The race antagonisms that blew up in the mid-1960s, the near-bankruptcy that sandbagged New York in the mid-1970s, the inadequate performance of the public

casing the cocktail party crowd, bouncing from affaire to affaire with an army of trainers and therapists to provide physical and psychological makeovers as needed. Tomorrow was never just another day; it was a bigger, better opportunity. There would be another model being photographed in the park, another film-shoot in process on the block. New friends and new relationships beckoned by the minute. If

INTRODUCTION

the smartest, and the coolest. They speak in superlatives, sure that New York is the biggest and the best; its ideas and products shape the world—and the world persuades them this is true.

The Twin Towers silently voiced it all. They caught and reflected the city's optimism and energy. Though massive, they were lean and clean enough in proportion and style to win general acceptance. Leave the pinnacles and spires and filigreed elegance to older cities; New York projects power and purpose. By 1980, everyone had forgotten that the World Trade Center had been a hotly debated project, that during the 1960s construction had been a slow, disruptive process, and that in the 1970s renting the new space had been difficult. That was the past; New York lived in the present, dreaming of the future. In the 1990s the

schools, the spiraling costs of housing, the lack of entry-level jobs, the increasing gap between rich and poor, and the city's slow strangulation by traffic—all persist. As for other big-city ills such as noise, dirt, poor air quality and incomprehensible tongues, New Yorkers simply take them for granted. "This is New York—the world's most exciting city. Whatever the problems, we can fix them," they persuade themselves. New Yorkers live for the new: the new job, the new apartment, lover, vacation, restaurant, show, movie, book. The economy and the city seem endlessly inventive; while one bubble burst, the next confidently swelled. New York could never be truly at risk.

The young professionals seem peerless and fearless; well-paid, well-groomed, ascending the corporate escalator, closing the deals,

life in London, Paris, Rome, Istanbul, New Delhi, Hong Kong and another half-dozen great cities was just as sophisticated and exciting as in New York, so what! New Yorkers discounted the claim. It had to be better here: this is New York!

But myth and reality and symbol and substance were beginning to separate even before the brilliant, sunny morning of September 11, 2001. The dot.com world was deflating like a punctured balloon. People who normally vacationed in Europe announced sudden, urgent needs to visit their parents in the Mid-West. The thin, nervy models were a little thinner and considerably more nervy, and the film-shoots on the streets served their crews bagels and cream cheese rather than brioches and imported jams. But New York still held reality at bay; this was merely a temporary

economic downturn, a useful correction; the system was shaking out the fat, tensing up for the next forward surge. Real trouble occurred only elsewhere; horrific events in Rwanda, in Serbia, in Bosnia and Kosovo; the frequent flare-ups in the Israel-Palestine confrontation and the occasional flare-ups in Northern Ireland were far away, almost unreal.

America remained blessed, beyond the reach of wars and shootings in the streets; Americans didn't have to listen to the day's death toll each evening on the TV news.

What New York and America lost on September 11, 2001 was not only thousands of innocent lives tragically ended, great buildings reduced to rubble and vibrant businesses blasted into bankruptcy. New York and America lost the deeply held myth of some peculiar, sacrosanct core of invincibility. Defying the horrific events of its own recent history, America had clung to this myth. New Yorkers managed to filter experience: the 1993 World Trade Center bombing had not brought the tower down; in the fullness of time the perpetrators were brought to justice.

The 1995 Oklahoma bombing was far more lethal, with 186 victims compared to six in the WTC bombing, but America assured itself this was a uniquely aberrational domestic crime, perpetrated by an American. The nation's mistake was to concentrate on the trials and the punishments of the perpetrators; the crime was to neglect the evidence of American vulnerability. In retrospect, it is clear that in September 2001 the intelligence and security systems maintained to protect New York and its bridges, tunnels, transportation, electrical and water supply were utterly inadequate.

Just what precautions can be taken and at what cost to a democratic nation's open society and civil liberties is hard to define. It would be easy enough in Tokyo, Beijing, Cairo or Riyadh to "keep an eye on foreigners" because they are so few and so identifiable. It's a different situation in European capitals with their broader mix of residents, and an even more different situation in major American cities, which have thoroughly mixed populations and remarkably few restrictions on activities or movement. Diversity and freedom are the blood and oxygen of American life.

On September 11, every American and most of the world's citizens realized an era had ended and life would thereafter be different. The nationwide response after the initial shock and the heroic rescue efforts says much for America. The instant solidarity felt between individuals in their communities and between the American people and their government, the refusal of individual Americans to ostracize Muslims, and the restraint Americans sought and their government has practiced in terms of retaliatory action all speak of great moral strength. The saving thought is that whatever the suffering now brought to Afghanistan, it will not equal the suffering that the Taliban continues to inflict.

It is a superb irony that many powerful Muslim critics of American government and policy live and work freely and untrammeled in America while in Muslim nations few critics of government remain free and at large for long. It's an irony too that the terrorists thrive only in the hinterlands of the least effectively governed Islamic nations, despised and condemned by thinking citizens. But a stronger, more immediate take on reality is to be found in asking a local Muslim cab driver, shish-kebab cart operator or newsstand owner in New York what he wants most. The answer very seldom has to do with American policy or Islam; it is most often the statement, "To bring the rest of my family to America."

Muslim immigrants willingly accept America with all her challenges. They are not afraid of hard work or raising families or taking on the risks of starting businesses; not afraid of naming their land of birth or practicing their religion. If they are afraid of anything, it is the remote possibility of being forced to return home. Their children move through the public schools and distinguish themselves in the nation's colleges and universities; they become Americans. Now for them and their parents, there is a fear: they may be at risk of death through the actions of their former countrymen who hate the nation that they, the successful immigrants, have come to love.

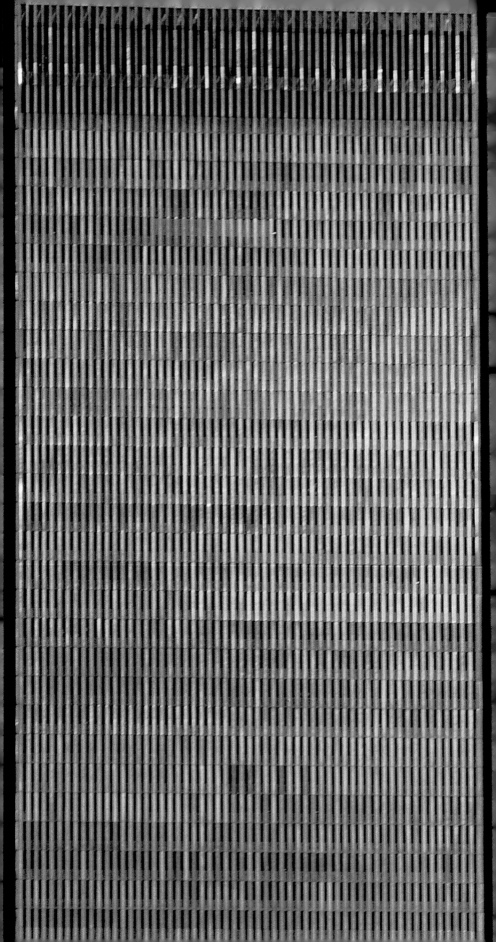

CHAPTER 1

MANHATTAN BEFORE
THE TWIN TOWERS

To picture New York and its life before the Twin Towers requires revisiting the 1960s, the decade before the towers were built. They were completed more than thirty years ago; the North Tower's first tenants moved in 1970 and the South Tower's did so in 1971. For a majority of New Yorkers and tristate area residents the Twin Towers have always been there, always visible, a lodestar and an undeniable fact of life. It takes conscious effort of will to conjure up the New York of the 1960s; recapturing the state and texture of the city demands more than just recalling the exuberant youth rebellion, the rock-and-roll highlights and the superficial 'good times glow' of that decade, especially its middle years. It requires searching for the underlying realities: the who-was-who among political leaders, the state of the economy, race relations, public services, education, and housing; it means examining perceptions about crime and public safety, about the quality of life and levels of confidence. For most people under forty the 1960s decade was before their time, ancient history they never shared. For those over sixty, it's "the old days," when life was different, more manageable—a time now slipping away in the haze of overburdened memory.

In 1960 John F. Kennedy was president, Nelson Rockefeller was governor of New York State, and Robert F. Wagner was mayor of New York. They were a trio of big, confident leaders in a big, bold decade. But it was a difficult, demanding decade in which prosperity and an exuberant

youth culture often seemed to be forces designed to keep people's minds off disasters. The Vietnam War and student protest, the assassination of President Kennedy, race riots and cities on fire, and then on to Watergate . . . Yet it remained a surprisingly optimistic decade—and New York did not seem to take its problems too seriously.

New York did not lack for iconic buildings before the Twin Towers soared 1,360 feet up from their Plaza into the heavens. Solid, vibrant Rockefeller Center, largely completed in the 1930s, with its mall and flag-studded sunken Plaza, was a major attraction, awash with New Yorkers and tourists. The city was affectionately proud of the Chrysler and Empire State buildings, both in midtown, rising high above their neighbors to dominate the skyline. The former (completed in 1930 and 1,046 ft high) was famous for its stainless-steel eagle heads, art deco trim and its 71st floor visitors' center; the latter (completed in 1931 and 1,250 ft high) offered an immensely popular observation deck. Both had ideal locations. The Chrysler building is only a block from Grand Central Terminal where the railway network serves the northern suburbs, and the Empire State building is conveniently close to Penn Station, with rail service to Long Island and New Jersey.

These two monumental stations have cautionary histories. Penn Station, modeled on the baths of Caracalla in Rome, was completed in 1911. In 1965, real estate interests

26 TOP
BATTERY PARK AND THE STATEN ISLAND FERRY TERMINAL IN THE 1940S.

27
THE 15-ACRE WTC SITE IN THE MID-1960S, BEFORE BUILDING DEMOLITIONS. THE AREA LACKED MAJOR ECONOMIC IMPORTANCE AND ARCHITECTURALLY SIGNIFICANT BUILDINGS, BUT WAS HOME TO HUNDREDS OF SMALL BUSINESSES, INCLUDING THE FAMOUS "RADIO ROW" OF ELECTRONICS DEALERS, AS WELL AS RESTAURANTS, BARS AND OTHER RETAIL ESTABLISHMENTS. OWNERS AND RESIDENTS PUT UP A FIERCE "SMALL MAN VS JUGGERNAUT" FIGHT BEFORE UNWILLINGLY LEAVING.

demolished it and built a bland office tower and covered arena. Only an intensely spirited public protest led by Jacqueline Bouvier Kennedy saved the magnificent Grand Central Terminal, completed in 1913 and famed for its vast, barrel-roofed Main Concourse, from a similar fate. Grand Central, now totally restored to its former splendor, is a visitors' "must see" destination, drawing millions annually.

Downtown in Lower Manhattan's Financial District, to the southeast of the Twin Towers' site, the 66-story Woolworth Building ("The Cathedral of Commerce," completed 1913) rose in relative isolation at Broadway and Park Place, a proud architectural icon, admired for its elegant masonry and terracotta cladding. The building looked across at City Hall (1812), a refined, cupola-topped two-story pavilion in a tree-filled park, and just south of it, to the bulkier, recently restored Victorian-classical Tweed Court House (1878). The three buildings are distinguished standouts of fine architecture, though a number of handsome older stone-clad office buildings keep them company. All could afford to be scornful of the banal new office towers plugged into to every possible site, particularly toward Wall Street and the south. To the casual visitor or the fast-moving tourist, New York seemed to be on wave of prosperity, enjoying boom times. The truth was far different; the city was entering stormy financial waters and within a decade would be poised on the brink of bankruptcy.

28-29
GOVERNORS ISLAND (LEFT FOREGROUND), ex-U.S. COAST GUARD HQ, IS AVAILABLE FOR $1 (WITH EXPENSIVE CONDITIONS). MOST OF MANHATTAN'S HUDSON RIVER PASSENGER AND FREIGHT PIERS HAVE BEEN DEMOLISHED, VICTIMS OF RISING COSTS. TOP LEFT: GEORGE WASHINGTON BRIDGE, BOTTOM RIGHT, BROOKLYN BRIDGE; WITH MANHATTAN BRIDGE JUST NORTH. SOUTH OF BROOKLYN BRIDGE IS THE HISTORIC BROOKLYN HEIGHTS RESIDENTIAL AREA.

29
THE LOVER MANHATTAN SKYLINE SEEN THROUGH BROOKLYN BRIDGE'S SUSPENSION CABLES.

A major cause of the city's worsening financial plight was the 1965 federal and state mandate that the city pay 25 percent of its welfare and associated medical care costs, previously entirely met from state and federal sources. Other causes included liberal welfare policies that added recipients to the public assistance rolls and generous pay raises for the city's fast-growing unionized workforce. Between 1960 and 1970, New York's budget more than tripled to over $6 billion. To meet financial needs, the city borrowed money, incurring heavy repayment obligations. By 1971, when the second of the Twin Towers was

MANHATTAN BEFORE THE TWIN TOWERS

29

30 TOP AND 30-31
NEW "BOX" HIGH-RISES INTRUDE AMONG
OLDER, DECORATIVE SKYSCRAPERS.
FOREGROUND: THE 5-BAY STATEN ISLAND
FERRY TERMINAL—HOME OF THE FAMOUS
"5-CENT RIDE." MID-LEFT: THE CIRCULAR
CASTLE CLINTON (1807) IN BATTERY
PARK, ONCE GUARDING NEW YORK
HARBOR.

31 BOTTOM RIGHT
PRESIDENT AND MRS. KENNEDY, SEEN IN
AN OPEN MOTORCADE ON LOWER
BROADWAY, WERE WARMLY WELCOMED
VISITORS TO NEW YORK. TICKER-TAPE
PARADES WERE RESERVED FOR SPORTS
VICTORIES OR FOREIGN HEADS OF STATE,
THOUGH IN 1960, JFK ENJOYED ONE AS A
PRESIDENTIAL CANDIDATE.

completed, the city was headed for financial disaster, with longer term loan repayment costs exceeding its current budget.

No remedies were in sight: property taxes had been hiked to the bearable maximum and new taxes added to business and personal income. As a result, businesses and residents were beginning to leave New York for more welcoming financial climates. Thus the gleaming Twin Towers, with 10 million square feet of brand-new office space, rose over a city is precipitous decline.

Though clear to the well informed, the city's rapidly worsening financial situation remained happily masked to millions of citizens and visitors. "Urban renewal," meaning a building boom, was a catchword; new office towers and apartment buildings were rising. The construction of Lincoln Center for the Performing Arts was underway, projected to be not only a cultural center but also a new anchor and catalyst for economic revival of the West Side between 59th and 72nd streets. Philharmonic Hall

(later renamed Avery Fisher Hall) opened in 1962, New York State Theater in 1964, and the Metropolitan Opera House in 1966. Much emphasis was given to the central Plaza that opened on to these first three Lincoln Center buildings. It was a welcoming public meeting place, a civic amenity, reflecting the marriage of the arts and life. The sight of the Plaza thronged with lively crowds from midday to mid-evening was not lost on the World Trade Center's planners and architects.

Behind the glitter and below the surface, New York was experiencing wrenching strains. The schools were seen as segregated and failing their minority students, and the educational bureaucracy was under heavy fire. "Experimental districts," with control by community school boards with parent participation, had led to a prolonged teacher strike. Concern existed that minorities were denied access to higher education, and in 1970 the city college system adopted a much criticized "open admissions" policy.

The Vietnam War had led to increasingly tense and disruptive demonstrations, and in 1968, student riots broke out at Columbia University over the university's collaboration with the Institute of Defense Analysis and its lack of support for community development in neighboring Harlem.

As the 1960s closed, the city was visibly in decline. The economy was weakening, public services were being cut, and the subways and commuter railroads were deteriorating. New York was no longer able to meet the reasonable needs of its minority citizens and their lot would worsen as the city faced an ever bleaker financial future. Given the overall situation, the majority of citizens welcomed the World Trade Center project. Yes, they said with a keen appraisal of reality, in the long run it would make the rich richer, but it had to be built, maintained and serviced, and that meant jobs—for some of them at least—and jobs meant income. All in all, building the Twin Towers was seen to be an act of confidence, heralding expectation of a brighter future for New York.

THE TWIN TOWERS:
DESIGN AND ARCHITECTURE

The Twin Towers no longer exist. For just thirty years they were the distinctive hallmark of the Manhattan skyline, one of the most famous in the world. More than an intrinsic visual reference point for downtown New York, the city's vital center, they were also the nerve center of the world economy. Yet their record-breaking height, structural design and the basic fact of their presence were always subject to criticism. It was never a secret that architectural critics did not fully support the World Trade Center project or the Twin Towers' size and design.

Two days after the September 11 attack on the Twin Towers, Nicolai Ouroussoff (the *Los Angeles Times'* architectural critic) described the construction of the towers as an act of optimism and outlined the unusually strong symbolism of the World Trade Center. At the same time, he referred to their "limited architectural value."

Richard Ingersoll (Professor of Architecture at Syracuse University in Florence, Italy; visiting professor at the Swiss Federal Institute of Technology, Zurich; founding editor of the *Design Book Review*) went further, claiming that the Twin Towers were a sad, dull place to work, and even considered that their vacuous forms were indicative of an imminent disaster. This negative opinion was not shared by ordinary people, who felt that the towers were a symbol not just of a city, but of an entire system; a liability, however, that the towers were saddled with from the day of their design.

In their book "Architettura Contemporanea" (Milan 1976), the authors and architectural historians Manfredo Tafuri and Francesco Dal Co discussed the WTC as a work that was "out of scale," and guilty of traumatically changing the development and functional balance of Manhattan.

A huge increase in the number of commuters was the project's first consequence, so significant that from 1966 on, Governor Nelson Rockefeller pushed for construction of a new city on the water—Battery Park City—with the aim of alleviating travel problems and exploiting the new skyscrapers' location. The initial 1966 plans for Battery Park City were by Wallace Harrison and his collaborators. In fact, according to Tafuri and Dal Co, Battery Park City, Roosevelt Island, and the World Trade Center together represented what Raymond Hood (1881-1934) had envisioned in his futuristic master plan, "Manhattan 1950." Discussion of the WTC project inevitably leads to its Japanese-American architect, Minoru Yamasaki (1912-1986),

assisted by Emory Roth, whose reputation was made by the WTC project. Architectural historians and critics prefer some of Yamasaki's other major works over the WTC. These include the St. Louis airport (1935-55), designed with G.F. Hellmuth and J. Leinweber (a terminal typified by a series of slender intersected cylindrical vaults covering the passenger waiting area), the Society of Arts and Crafts building (Detroit, 1958); the American Concrete Institute building (Detroit, 1959), or the Reynolds Metals Offices, also in Detroit (1959). The most typical elements of Yamasaki's work are vaults that mask structural elements of the walls, often formed by profiled modules made from concrete or other agglomerates.

After studying architecture at the universities in Washington and New York, Yamasaki worked for Shreve, Lamb and Harmon—the architects of the Empire State Building—where perhaps the idea was born and nursed that, one day, he could compete with the masters. The masters Yamasaki most admired were Mies van der Rohe and Le Corbusier.

The WTC was conceived in 1962, began to take form in 1964, and the first construction started in 1966. The towers' distinctive features were geometric divisions, glass walls, and load-bearing

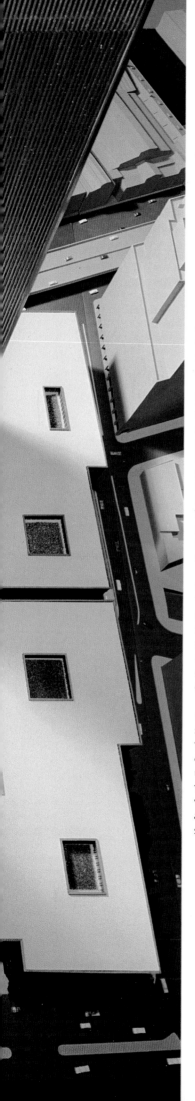

columns. The North Tower was completed in 1971, and the South in 1974, when the WTC complex was inaugurated.

Strongly promoted by the Port Authority of New York and New Jersey, the WTC was a sensational project for the period, aimed at bringing into being a commercial district of great visual impact in a depressed area. It occupied (it is sad to have to refer to it in the past tense) a total ground area of over 15 acres, and the Plaza at the base of the towers exceeded five acres in extent.

Yamasaki believed deeply in the project, stating, "The World Trade Center must . . . become the living representation of the faith of man in humanity, of his need for individual dignity, of his trust in co-operation and, through this, of his ability to find greatness."

The WTC's immense scale is reflected in the extraordinary statistics that describe the 10-year project, to use a rather dry term for a mighty undertaking. In addition to the towers (1 and 2 WTC) were five other buildings and an immense subterranean shopping mall. No. 3 WTC was

the Marriott Hotel (designed by Skidmore, Owings and Merrill, and built in 1971 as the Vista Hotel); 4 WTC housed the Commodities Exchange; 6 WTC was the 8-story U.S. Customs House. The remainder were office buildings. To a greater or lesser extent, all were destroyed by the collapse of the towers.

The Twin Towers were each roughly 1,360 feet high, 196 feet long on each side, had 110 floors and 104 elevators. They rested on foundations that penetrated 69 feet into the bedrock. Construction required 200,000 tons of steel and 3,000 miles of electrical cable to satisfy the daily distribution and consumption of about 80,000 kilowatts. For express elevator ascent, the structures were divided into three vertical zones. The towers had over 43,000 windows, each one 22 inches wide. In total, the façades required some 215,000 square feet of glass.

The initial stage was the clearance and excavation of 12,000,000 square feet of land, with the preservation

40-41
THE WORLD TRADE CENTER MODEL
REVEALS THE HUGE SIZE OF THE PLAZA
(APPROXIMATELY 5 ACRES) THAT LIES AT
THE FOOT OF THE TOWERS, AND THE
"NORMAL" HEIGHT OF THE OTHER
BUILDINGS IN THE COMPLEX.

41 TOP
THE PORT AUTHORITY OF NEW YORK AND
NEW JERSEY WAS INITIATOR AND MOVING
FORCE BEHIND THE CONSTRUCTION OF THE
WTC. SEEN HERE IS THE ENTRANCE TO
THE PA'S INFORMATION OFFICE.

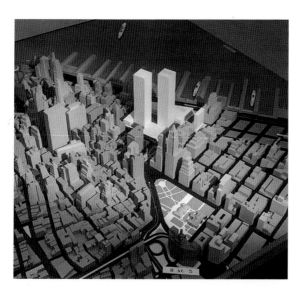

(and re-routing) of the New York-New Jersey subterranean railway lines, and accommodation for the New York subway and pedestrian passageways.

Yamasaki produced about one hundred models before choosing the two towers, which represented a breakthrough configuration compromise. This option offered the possibility of creating the required ten million square feet of office space. In designing the towers, Yamasaki went beyond the existing principles of skyscraper construction (the U.S.'s most important contribution to architecture), making skillful use of technology and materials.

The structural system was simple and effective. The façades (196 ft wide) were to all effects a cage made of steel and prefabricated sections (in modules measuring 10 x 32 feet), able to resist wind-induced and seismic strains without transferring stress to the towers' core structure, but distributing and absorbing it throughout the outer wall structure. The structures were highly resistant yet light, without internal columns beyond the elevator core.

Designed to resist atmospheric agents, seismic events and even accidental intrusion (including being hit by an airliner), the Twin Towers were unable to withstand the heat caused by flaming combustion of the 20,000 gallons of jet fuel spilt into each tower on September 11. The heat literally detached the concrete-clad floors from the towers' steel core and exterior walls. These, having lost their characteristics of resistance and flexibility because of excessive heat, gave way under the weight of the structure.

It is certainly right, though perhaps a little premature, to consider a future for the WTC site and to document the unexpected argument that pits supporters of the creation of a memorial against the faction of "rebuilders." Renzo Piano, who was recently received a commission to design the New York Times' new midtown offices, states that he favors construction of new skyscrapers, though perhaps not so high—only 656 feet.

The proposal by two artists and two architects (Julian La Verdière and Paul Myoda; John Bennet and Gustavo Monteverdi) is more spectacular and verges on kitsch; their idea is the temporary creation of two towers of light, the diaphanous representation of what used to stand on the site.

More simply and realistically, what remains of one of the most famous, debated and daring projects of American—or even world—architecture is the knowledge of its absence, its memory and the warning it provides.

44

A LARGE SCALE MODEL WAS SET OUT FOR A PHOTOGRAPHIC SESSION. BASED ON A HUMAN SCALE, THE SIZE OF THE PRE-EXISTING BUILDINGS AND THE MAJESTY OF THE TOWERS ARE CLEARLY EVIDENT; ONCE ERECTED, THEY WOULD DOMINATE THE SURROUNDING BUILDINGS FROM AN IMMENSE HEIGHT.

45

THE *DEUS EX MACHINA* OF A PROJECT ABOUT TO BE SET IN MOTION, ARCHITECT MINORU YAMASAKI'S THOUGHTS ARE PROBABLY DIVIDED BETWEEN THE KNOWLEDGE OF A SUCCESSFUL DESIGN AND THE CHALLENGE OF EXECUTION, WITH THE INEVITABLE ADJUSTMENTS AND UNEXPECTED PROBLEMS THAT WILL EMERGE DURING CONSTRUCTION. IT TOOK 8 YEARS FROM THE START OF THE EXCAVATION IN 1966 TO THE INAUGURATION IN 1973, BUT THE WORLD TRADE CENTER BEGAN ITS INDEPENDENT WORKING LIFE AS EARLY AS 1971.

DESIGN AND ARCHITECTURE

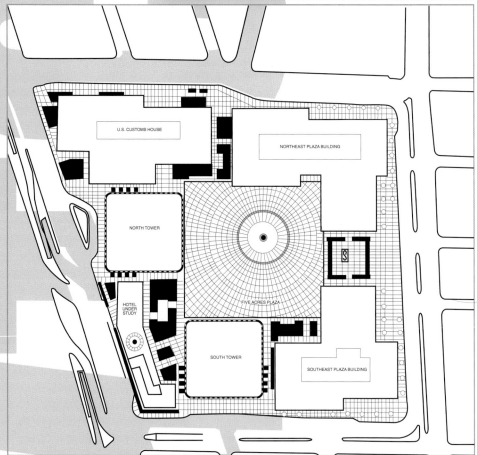

U.S. CUSTOMS HOUSE

NORTHEAST PLAZA BUILDING

NORTH TOWER

FIVE ACRES PLAZA

HOTEL UNDER STUDY

SOUTH TOWER

SOUTHEAST PLAZA BUILDING

46 TOP
IN THIS VIEW OF THE MODEL, THE PLAZA
OF THE COMPLEX, THOUGH ENORMOUS,
SEEMS TO HAVE BEEN SACRIFICED AND
TRAMPLED BY THE MASSIVE BULK OF THE
TOWERS.

46 BOTTOM
PERHAPS THE PAVING OF THE PLAZA—
SHOWN HERE IN PLAN—WAS SUPPOSED TO
MITIGATE THE INSISTENTLY ORTHOGONAL
DESIGN OF THE COMPLEX.

47
THE MODEL CLEARLY SHOWS THE TOWERS'
THREE MODULES. THEY WERE CHOSEN
FROM OVER ONE HUNDRED MODELS AS THE
IDEAL MORPHOLOGICAL COMPROMISE.

48-49
OVER 66 FEET OF ROCK HAD TO BE
REMOVED TO PROVIDE SUFFICIENT
FOUNDATIONS TO ANCHOR THE TOWERS TO
THE GROUND. THE APOCALYPTIC PIT SHOWN
HERE CONTAINS THE FRAMEWORK
NECESSARY FOR THE EXCAVATION TO BE
ACCOMPLISHED.

48 BOTTOM
ALL THE POWER LINES, AIR INLETS AND
TELEPHONE CABLES RAN BENEATH EACH
FLOOR. THE BUILDINGS WERE EQUIPPED
WITH COMPLEX HEATING AND ENERGY
MANAGEMENT SYSTEMS THAT WERE
EXTREMELY MODERN FOR THE ERA.

49 BOTTOM
ANOTHER CITY LAY BENEATH THE WORLD
TRADE CENTER: IT COMPRISED CAR PARKS,
SUBWAY AND RAILWAY LINES, MILES OF
CABLES AND THE MASSIVE MACHINERY
NEEDED TO MAINTAIN THE VERTICAL
METROPOLIS IN OPERATION.

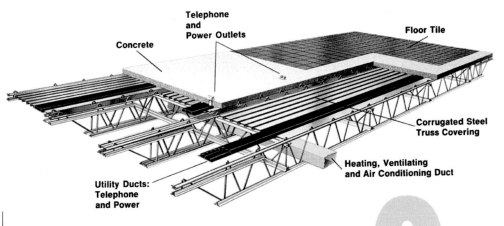

Concrete

Telephone and Power Outlets

Floor Tile

Corrugated Steel Truss Covering

Heating, Ventilating and Air Conditioning Duct

Utility Ducts: Telephone and Power

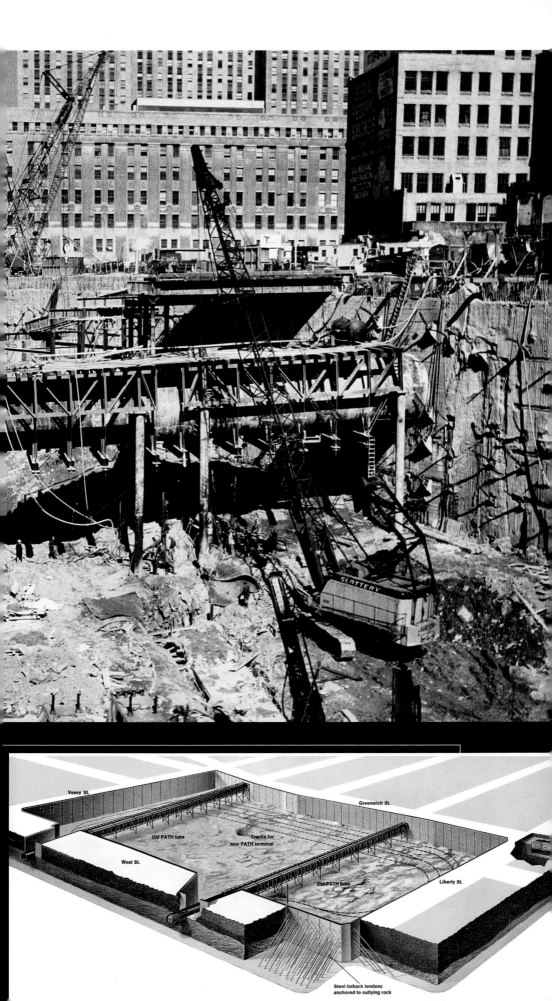

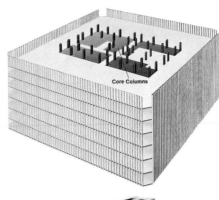

Core Columns

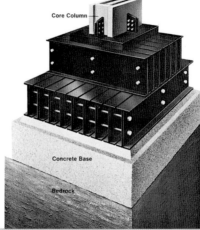

Core Column

Concrete Base

Bedrock

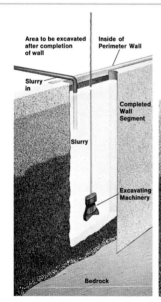

Area to be excavated after completion of wall

Inside of Perimeter Wall

Slurry in

Slurry

Completed Wall Segment

Excavating Machinery

Bedrock

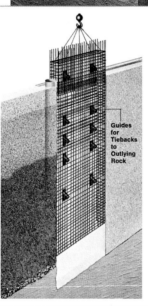

Guides for Tiebacks to Outlying Rock

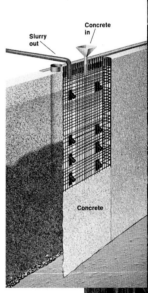

Slurry out

Concrete in

Concrete

50 TOP
THIS VIEW SHOWS THE STEEL LOAD-BEARING
STRUCTURE OF THE TOWERS AND THE
ANCHORING OF THE METAL COLUMNS TO THE
PLINTH MADE OF REINFORCED CONCRETE.

50 CENTER
THE STEEL MODULES (EACH MEASURING
10X33 FEET) EMERGE FROM THE BEDROCK TO
SUPPORT THE TWIN TOWERS—THE WORLD'S
TALLEST BUILDINGS AT THE TIME OF THE
PROJECT'S INAUGURATION.

50 BOTTOM
THESE DRAWINGS SHOW THE PHASES OF
EXCAVATION, INSERTION OF THE REINFORCING
FRAMEWORK, AND THE FINAL CASTING OF
THE FOUNDATIONS OF THE PERIMETER WALLS.

50-51
THIS PHOTO GIVES A GOOD INDICATION OF
THE DEPTH OF THE FOUNDATIONS. ON THE
RIGHT ARE THE PERIMETER WALLS; ON THE
LEFT THE STEEL FRAMEWORK IS BEING BUILT.

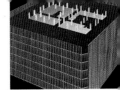

52-53
The construction system for the Twin Towers is clearly shown here: a support core, the elevator shafts and plants, and the strong "self-supporting" perimeter framework.

53 top
The bare structure of the steel framework has not yet been covered with the uninterrupted rows of small windows (only 22 inches wide); they will give an impression of harmonized strength and flexibility.

53 center
This drawing clearly shows how the prefabricated sections of the floors rested on both the central core and the strong perimeter sections.

53 bottom
A moment during the anchoring of the steel modules by skilled steel erectors accustomed to working on high-rise towers.

54-55
A STRIKING PHOTOGRAPH OF LOWER
MANHATTAN WITH THE NOT YET
COMPLETED TOWERS ALREADY DECLARING
THEIR IMPOSING PRESENCE. THEIR ACRES
OF WINDOWS WOULD HAVE BEEN
SUFFICIENT FOR THE NEEDS OF A TOWN OF
10,000 INHABITANTS.

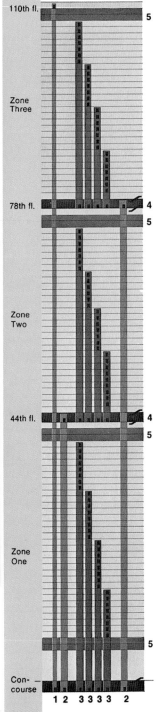

110th fl. — 5

Zone
Three

78th fl. — 4
— 5

Zone
Two

44th fl. — 4
— 5

Zone
One

— 5

Con-
course

1 2 3 3 3 3 2

55 TOP
THE VERTICAL THRUST OF THE FAÇADE
CLEARLY SHOWS THE HORIZONTAL SECTION
BREAKS AT 1/3RD AND AGAIN AT 2/3RDS OF
HEIGHT. YAMASAKI'S DESIGN CALLED FOR
THE TOWERS TO BE MADE UP OF THREE
ALMOST IDENTICAL SECTIONS.

55 BOTTOM
THE THREE-SECTION STRUCTURE WAS ALSO
REFLECTED IN THE ARRANGEMENT OF THE
SUPERFAST ELEVATORS
(104 IN EACH TOWER).

59
IN THIS PHOTO TAKEN AT THE BEGINNING OF
THE 1980S, THE TWIN TOWERS ARE
REFLECTED IN THE WATERS OF THE HUDSON:
NO OTHER STRUCTURES HAVE YET BEEN BUILT
BETWEEN THEM AND THE RIVERFRONT.

60-61
THE POINTED ARCHES THAT DISTINGUISHED
THE LOWER PORTION OF THE BUILDINGS WERE
PROBABLY THE ONLY DECORATIVE ELEMENTS
THAT YAMASAKI WANTED TO GRANT
THE TOWERS.

56
IN THIS BIRD'S EYE VIEW OF THE WORLD
TRADE CENTER THE TOWERS DOMINATE
THE PLAZA AND THE OTHER BUILDINGS OF
THE COMPLEX.

57 TOP
THE PLAZA AT THE EXACT MOMENT THE
SHADOW OF THE SOUTH TOWER IS
THROWN ONTO THE CORNER OF THE
NORTH TOWER TO CREATE A FASCINATING
PLAY OF LIGHT.

57 CENTER AND BOTTOM
THE WORLD TRADE CENTER IS COMPLETE:
THE YEAR IS 1973 (AS THE CLOTHES WORN
TO THE INAUGURATION CEREMONY
SUGGEST). NOTE THAT THE LANDFILL IN
THE HUDSON RIVER, ON WHICH THE
WORLD FINANCIAL CENTER WILL BE BUILT,
IS STILL EMPTY.

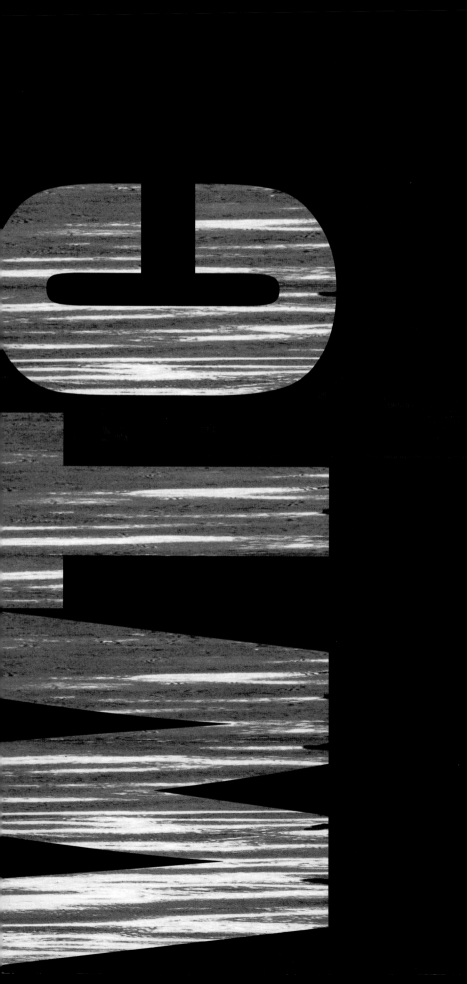

Legend:

■ Collapsed buildings
□ Partly collapsed buildings
▨ Buildings with major damage
▨ Buildings with structural damage
▨ Buildings damaged but stable, ready for occupancy with repairs/cleaning
▨ Buildings which need cleaning
□ Buildings not affected

MAP OF DISASTER AREA

COLLAPSED BUILDINGS:
1 - 1 WORLD TRADE CENTER
2 - 2 WORLD TRADE CENTER
3 - 7 WORLD TRADE CENTER
4 - 5 WORLD TRADE CENTER
5 - NORTH BRIDGE

PARTLY COLLAPSED BUILDINGS:
6 - 6 WORLD TRADE CENTER
7 - MARRIOTT HOTEL
8 - 4 WORLD TRADE CENTER
9 - ONE LIBERTY PLAZA

BUILDINGS WITH MAJOR DAMAGE:
10 - EAST RIVER SAVINGS BANK
11 - FEDERAL BUILDING
12 - 3 WORLD FINANCIAL CENTER
13 - ST. NICHOLAS CHURCH
14 - 90 WEST STREET
15 - BANKERS TRUST
16 - SOUTH BRIDGE

BUILDINGS WITH STRUCTURAL DAMAGE:
17 - MILLENNIUM HILTON
18 - 2 WORLD FINANCIAL CENTER
19 - 1 WORLD FINANCIAL CENTER
20 - 30 WEST BROADWAY
21 - WINTER GARDEN
22 - N.Y. TELEPHONE BUILDING
23 - 4 WORLD FINANCIAL CENTER

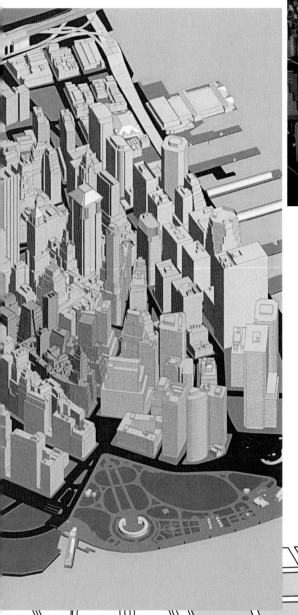

62-63 AND 63 BOTTOM
THE AXONOMETRIC VIEW SHOWN HERE
(WITH THE PLAN TO THE RIGHT) SHOWS
THE SITUATION BEFORE AND AFTER THE
ATTACK ON SEPTEMBER 11. A SURPRISING
NUMBER OF NEARBY BUILDINGS SUFFERED
SEVERE STRUCTURAL DAMAGE.

63 TOP RIGHT
THE NEW WORLD FINANCIAL CENTER IS
COMPLETE. DESIGNED BY CÉSAR PELLI
(1981-1987), THE TOWERS ROSE ON
LANDFILL IN THE HUDSON RIVER, JUST
WEST OF THE WORLD TRADE CENTER AND
ADJOINING BATTERY PARK CITY.

64-65 AND 65 BOTTOM RIGHT
LOWER MANHATTAN AS IT APPEARED FROM
OVERHEAD JUST BEFORE AND AFTER THE
TERRIBLE ATTACK ON SEPTEMBER 11.

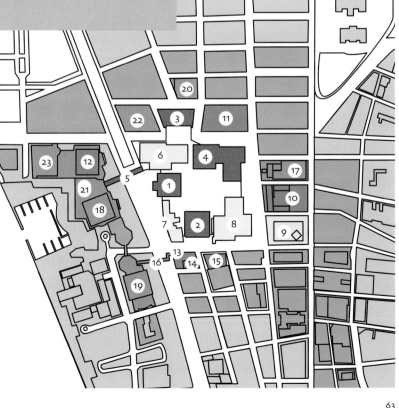

world tra

GTD

WTO

A CATALYST FOR CREATIVITY

CHAPTER 3

68

MAY, 1983. LIKE GEORGE WILLIG, DANIEL
GOODWIN CLIMBED THE NORTH TOWER.
LUCKILY, NEW YORKERS DID NOT FOLLOW
SUIT WHOLESALE.

69

130 FEET TO GO; 1,350 FEET TO FALL . . .
ON AUGUST 7, 1974, PHILIPPE PETIT
CAPTURED THE WORLD'S ADMIRATION WITH
HIS DARING FEAT. HIS CONFIDENCE WAS
BORN OF PROFESSIONALISM AND
PREPARATION.

The Twin Towers became instant icons. Almost all architectural critics and propounders of the higher aesthetic condemned or dismissed them, often as casually as the public dismisses critics. The towers were too brash, too big, and too dominant, shattering the urban scale, overburdening the area. But New Yorkers on the whole admired the Twin Towers as quintessential examples of the city's "can do" energy and reflections of their own enthusiasm for the best and the newest—even if it had to be the biggest. An additional factor played a role in humanizing the Twin Towers. Three events occurring within five years, each unique in New York's history, endowed the Twin Towers with a special mystique, a magnetism that made New Yorkers realize the towers challenged the human imagination. The towers themselves had entered the record book with a plethora of 'firsts.' Now, by simply existing, they caused new 'firsts' to happen and enter the record.

The first event occurred on August 7, 1974, when New Yorkers left home for work to the surprising news that Philippe Petit, a 24-year-old French citizen, had successfully secured a tightrope between the towers and had made several elegant and seemingly carefree crossings. Contemporary reports made it clear that the PA, New York police and the public had experienced much anxiety—and that Philippe Petit had not.

The second event occurred a little over a year later, on July 22, 1975. That morning Owen Quinn, a 24-year-old New Yorker, made a parachute jump from the roof of the North Tower. Though quickly executed and not unduly complicated, Quinn's jump was dramatic and not without danger. After his safe but bruising landing, the Port Authority charged him with criminal trespass, concerned to discourage other risk-takers. The move did not succeed. On May 26, 1977, another New Yorker, George Willig, aged 27, achieved an exciting first. Using clamps that he had designed to lock into grooves in the tower's façade, he made a three-hour ascent from base to rooftop, a time-span that greatly pleased the media and enthralled a worldwide audience.

Almost effortlessly the Twin Towers promoted themselves. The five-acre Plaza from which they rose was a pedestrian haven removed from vehicular traffic, its focal point a vast fountain and massive bronze spherical sculpture whose sweeping curve was in dramatic contrast to the unbroken vertical lines of the towers. A full calendar of planned and impromptu events—music, theater and other—made the Plaza a place of endlessly changing scenes. The Plaza, bigger than the Piazza of San Marco in Venice, was a natural starting point for pleasurable activity. Beyond it was the bridge to the World Financial Center and the Winter Garden, opening onto the Marina and

the Battery Park City Esplanade and the Hudson River. To the south rose the familiar New York Harbor icon, the Statue of Liberty. Below the Plaza was the Concourse, a permanent magnet for the compulsive shopper.

Two predictable but rewarding features drew visitors and New Yorkers alike to the Twin Towers. The enclosed observation deck on the 107th floor of the South Tower, with its access to the roof, opened in December 1975 and became an instant hit. The deck did not overtake the Empire State Building's 86th-floor open-air observation terrace; fortunately, each offered the best vista in at least one direction. The World Trade Center's observation deck offered stunning views to the south, over New York Harbor and Brooklyn. From the Empire State Building's deck, Central Park unrolling to the north seems only a stone's throw away. Both attractions drew over 1.5 million paying viewers per year; neither complained of being edged out of the market.

In the North Tower, the fashionable *Windows on the World* restaurant on the 107th floor opened in April 1976, and quickly became renowned for an imaginative menu and an excellent wine list. For hundreds of thousands of New Yorkers and visitors, *Windows on the World* offered lunch with unrivalled panoramic views. Drinks and dinner à deux there, above the city's myriad lights, with the Staten

70-71 AND 71
"THE SPHERE," A 27-FOOT-HIGH BRONZE
SCULPTURE, WAS THE FOCAL POINT OF THE
TWIN TOWERS' 5-ACRE PLAZA. THE
GERMAN SCULPTOR FRITZ KOENIG
DESIGNED THE MUCH-ADMIRED WORK.

Island ferries crossing the black waters below like programmed fireflies, was the launching-pad for countless memorable romances.

On the movie front the Twin Towers quickly reached the screen. The 1976 remake of "King Kong" (first filmed in 1933), had as its unforgettable climax a hunted King Kong leaping from tower to tower, a terrified Jessica Lange clutched in his mighty paw, moments before his fatal plunge. For once, the Empire State Building was dramatically upstaged. Because New York and Lower Manhattan are perennially popular locations for shooting movies, the Twin Towers appeared on screen time and time again, if only in fleeting exterior shots. Practical considerations, security issues and cost made it very difficult to set up and shoot within the towers, though they feature prominently in mock-up or reality in a number of films. Among the better known are Woody Allen's nostalgic "Manhattan" (1979, Diane Keaton, Meryl Streep); "Escape from New York" (1981, Kurt Russell), featuring the towers in a futuristic horror movie; "Wall Street" (1987, Michael Douglas and Charlie Sheen); and "Working Girl" (1988, Sigourney Weaver and Harrison Ford), in which the ambitious Melanie Griffith gazes up at the Twin Towers, a symbol of unbounded ambition, a salute to success. "Godzilla" (1998, Mathew Broderick and Maria Pitilli) was a return to the fantastic.

By 1980 the Twin Towers image was undeniably entrenched in the public mind, and its use has never lessened. Channel 11, a major New York TV station, adapted the Twin Towers' profile and adopted the design as a logo, placing it on countless TV screens day in and day out. Liquor companies, including Maker's Mark Bourbon and Bacardi Rum, have used the image in high-profile advertising campaigns; numerous other companies have featured the Twin Towers on merchandise or on shopping bags or promotions. Fine photography has captured the Twin Towers from endless angles; vertical candles in the dusk cut by the curving light-laced horizontal of Brooklyn Bridge, or rising across the Harbor, above and beyond Lady Liberty's familiar high-held torch, or in closer shots, framing the classic façade of St. Paul's Chapel.

Approaching Lower Manhattan from New Jersey, from Staten Island, from Brooklyn or Long Island, the Twin Towers dominate the skyline. They are never just there; they are powerfully, strikingly there. Seen from the Brooklyn Heights Esplanade,

the Twin Towers become almost magical. They shimmer in the brilliant morning light of a spring day; at dusk in winter they are pillars of light in a darkened sky.

And now the Twin Towers and so much else around them are gone; utterly destroyed in a psychopathic act of mindless hatred. Without doubt, new buildings will rise. Some suggest a memorial within a park; others ask for housing; still others suggest a defiant rebuilding of the WTC and Twin Towers complex. The economic, demographic, employment, and transportation calculus is vastly changed from that of the 1970s; whatever is built must be governed by sensitive interpretation of new criteria.

It is too soon to invest in plans and schedules: the current chapter is not yet closed; the tragedy is too recent and too raw. But what the WTC stood for cannot, must not, be forgotten. Minoru Yamasaki, the quiet, thoughtful architect of the World Trade Center, captured that purpose in words that will not be surpassed:

"World trade means world peace and consequently the World Trade Center buildings in New York. . . had a bigger purpose than just to provide room for tenants. The World Trade Center is a living symbol of man's dedication to world peace. . . beyond the compelling need to make this a monument to world peace, the World Trade Center should, because of its importance, become a representation of man's belief in humanity, his need for individual dignity, his belief in the cooperation of men, and through cooperation, his ability to find greatness."

CHAPTER

74
HELEN FRANKENTHALER, A NEW YORK
PAINTER GREATLY ADMIRED AS AN ABSTRACT
EXPRESSIONIST, EXECUTED THIS STRIKING MAJOR
WORK, MOUNTED IN THE TOWER LOBBY.

75
ONE QUARTER OF A TWIN TOWER WRAP-
AROUND LOBBY, WITH THE ELEVATOR CORE
AT LEFT. OPENNESS AND SPACIOUSNESS
WERE KEY DESIGN ELEMENTS THROUGHOUT
THE WTC; HENCE THE 10-STORY LOBBY.

76 BOTTOM
"MEET YOU IN THE WINDOWS ON THE
WORLD!" A GREAT NEW YORK
EXPERIENCE: DESIGN, DÉCOR, FOOD, WINE,
MOOD AND MOMENT CAME TRIUMPHANTLY
TOGETHER. IF WORDS FAILED, THERE WAS
ALWAYS THE VIEW . . .

76-77
THE WINTER GARDEN ADDED WHIMSICAL
ELEGANCE TO THE TRADE AND FINANCIAL
CENTERS, AND DRAMATIC LIGHTING ADDED
TO ITS MANY SPECIAL EVENTS. THE PALM
TREES HAVE SEEN IT ALL . . .

78 AND 79
FILMING "KING KONG"
(JOHN GUILLERMIN, 1976) CALLED
FOR CROWD SCENES, PARTICULARLY
IN DYING KONG'S FALL TO THE PLAZA.
NEW YORKERS JUST LOVED BEING PART
OF THE ACTION . . .

80 AND 81
IN "INDEPENDENCE DAY," ALIENS FROM
OUTER SPACE CAST A GIANT SHADOW,
THREATENING THE TWIN TOWERS,
NEW YORK AND THE NATION.
THE DUO OF "TOUGH GUYS" WHO SAVED
THE UNITED STATES IN "MEN IN BLACK"
SEEMED TO BE FEARLESS BEFORE
THE ALIEN THREAT.

A CATALYST FOR CREATIVITY

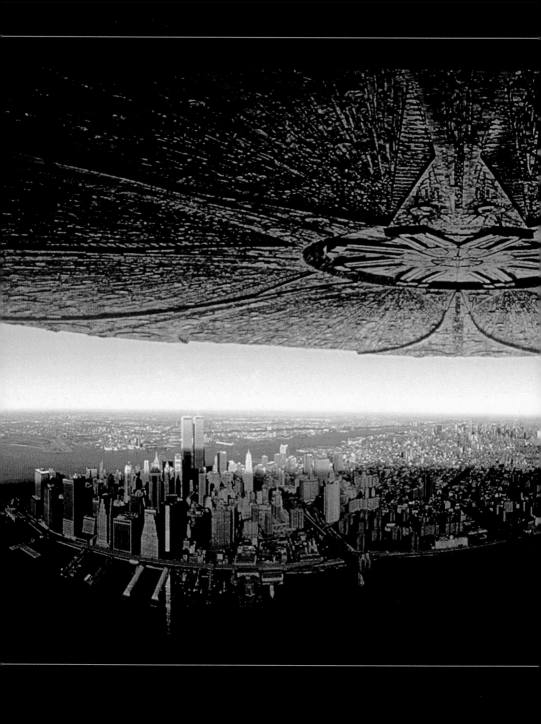

PROTECTING
THE EARTH
FROM THE SCUM
OF THE
UNIVERSE

world tra

WTO

THE NEW HEART OF
THE FINANCIAL DISTRICT

Over its thirty-year life span, the World Trade Center—the Twin Towers and the five smaller buildings, including the Marriott Hotel—was a driving force in the revitalization of Lower Manhattan and the Financial District. For hundreds of millions throughout the world, the Twin Towers symbolized the power of American capitalism. But that was not the primary goal, and it's important to remember who financed and built the WTC, what its original purpose was, and how through natural synergies that purpose expanded and changed.

Ironically enough, the brilliant, bold, and hugely successful idea for the WTC came from a powerful but low-profile government agency that financed itself from airport and marine terminal user fees and from bridge and tunnel tolls, accruing large surpluses that it needed to invest. The agency was the Port Authority of New York and New Jersey (the PA), founded in 1921 to "improve trade and commerce." At first, the PA's main activity was operating marine cargo ports on the New York-New Jersey waterfronts. In the 1930s the PA built the George Washington Bridge across the Hudson, linking New York and New Jersey. It also operated the existing airports, and after World War II built new and vastly bigger ones. By the late 1950s, maritime trade became more competitive and less expansionary. New York felt the squeeze; almost all the docks were to close down by the 1960s, the victim of crowded access streets, expensive warehousing and trucking, and high labor costs. On the New Jersey side, the dock environment was more favorable and the PA was more aggressive, building Port Elizabeth and Port Newark in the late 1940s-early 1950s as new, high efficiency, fast turnaround docks for huge container ships and tankers.

At the beginning of the 1960s, the PA had money and needed public-benefit projects on which to spend it. A trade center was one possibility, soon backed by the financial sector (the loosely allied banks, real estate tycoons, and major investors), which realized that a major new office complex would revitalize Lower Manhattan, an area within minutes of Wall Street. If the PA's financial resources met most or all of the costs, so much the better. If, in keeping with its charter to "improve commerce and trade," the PA brought in numerous businesses involved in these activities, so much the better; the situation between them and the Wall Street money men would be collaborative rather than competitive.

In the late 1960s the New York-New Jersey region was declining as a trade and shipping center, with Houston and New Orleans growing rapidly. New York needed a dramatic, high profile project to help it and the region recapture pre-eminence in trade and associated finance. Whole areas of the city were deteriorating; Lower Manhattan urgently needed revitalization, urban renewal had passed it by and decay was evident. The Hudson waterfront area to the northwest of Wall Street, was ripe for redevelopment, particularly some thirty blocks of old, low-rise small and mid-sized business buildings. A brand new World Trade Center for the export, import, shipping, insurance and financing communities could be a powerful catalyst for growth. In short, the World Trade Center was an idea whose time had come, and as such it drew powerful political and financial support.

Big projects meant big money, and everybody wanted a piece of the action. Hundreds of issues had to be resolved, including the size, scope, and governance of the project and its financing, land acquisition, design, transportation, and taxation. The states of New York and New Jersey and New York City had vested but differing interests and requirements. Wall Street, the banks, and the great financiers had differing and often competing interests.

Knowing that some industries and businesses would benefit and others might be hurt (including major real estate and office-

86 BOTTOM
THE VIEW ALONG THE WEST SIDE HIGHWAY
TOWARD THE WORLD FINANCIAL CENTER
CONFIRMS MANHATTAN'S TOTAL LOSS OF
PASSENGER AND FREIGHT SHIPPING.

86-87
THE WINTER GARDEN'S CURVILINEAR
STEEL-AND-GLASS CONSTRUCTION IS IN
DRAMATIC CONTRAST TO THE NORTH
TOWER'S VERTICAL MODULARITY.

leasing companies), powerful real estate, business and financial groups tried to shape the project. Among the voices of protest were small business owners, shopkeepers and residents who would be ousted. They were surprisingly effective in getting heard and winning sympathy, but the PA was a governmental entity with power of eminent domain— able to "buy" land from owners unwilling to sell. Thus owners and businesses were sacrificed to the juggernaut of "progress." Despite powerful criticism about the PA's entry into the commercial and real estate market places, New York and New Jersey, with an eye to economic benefits, passed the legislation that enabled the PA to proceed. They recognized that older office buildings were losing tenants to newer ones; some major financial and brokerage houses had moved to newer, more efficient and utilitarian buildings in Mid-Manhattan. The WTC would be the dynamo of the economic revival and urban renewal of Lower Manhattan, so the Twin Towers became a reality.

The World Trade Center never became what its name advertised and over time anticipation and actuality moved ever farther apart. For a decade or so the WTC courted maritime, trade, and related businesses, without ever becoming the single hub for them. New York State and the PA rented very substantial amounts of space; neither were remotely trade organizations. In the 1980s, WTC rents began to move from below-market to equal to or above-market rates. Smaller tenants left the WTC; banks, brokerage houses, insurance companies and law firms moved in, reflecting a wide-ranging mix with fewer trade companies.

With the Twin Towers unrivalled as the defining feature of the Manhattan skyline, and the busy, vibrant five-acre Plaza between the towers well established as a popular meeting place, the WTC began to replace Wall Street as the biggest tourist magnet in Lower Manhattan. Differentiations of roles and activities further blurred during the 1980s and 1990s. The establishment of the Commodities Exchange at 4 WTC and construction of the privately funded World Financial Center, immediately west of the WTC, further expanded the old Financial

District, traditionally centered on Wall Street and concentrated to the southeast. Increasingly, for younger New Yorkers and for tourists of all ages, the WTC typified the Financial District and was its visible, beating heart. Summer and winter alike visitors and tourists streamed across the covered bridge connecting the WTC to the World Financial Center. It was leisurely stroll down through the elegant crystal palace of the Winter Garden, out onto the Hudson River waterfront and to the parks and handsome esplanade that add amenity and elegance to the new apartment blocks of Battery Park City.

The standard circuit took visitors back across a second covered bridge and south to the narrow streets that lead over to Wall Street. Then it's back to the WTC and the vast shopping and dining Concourse below. There a huge range of stores, many of them decidedly fashionable, catered to every consumer whim. The air-conditioned Concourse became a place to visit in its own right; busy, exciting and offering every sort of culinary treat—a very comforting escapist world.

No resident or worker or visitor in the Financial District could for even a moment forget the soaring presence of the silvery, clean-lined Twin Towers. They and the adjoining buildings housed a vibrant community of more than 50,000 people from all over the world; the best, the brightest, and the most confident. In a thousand ways a day they made opportunity, created markets and business, and moved money and goods. Their presence and energy fueled a small world of restaurants and stores, bazaars and boutiques, cafes and conversations. Enthusiasm for life was palpable; walking across the Plaza in the sunny high noon of a perfect New York day or in a brilliantly lit early evening, the message in the air was: "Dream it; do it." It was a very fitting message. The World Trade Center began as an almost impossible dream: it became, if only briefly, a dream realized, a whole new world.

90-91 AND 91
THE GENEROUSLY SPACED YET SLENDER
VERTICALS IN THE TWIN TOWER LOBBIES
AND THE CONTRASTINGLY MUSCULAR
HORIZONTAL BANDS COMBINE TO SUGGEST
STRENGTH AND OPENNESS—A NECESSARY
ELEMENT CONSIDERING THE VAST HUMAN
FLOWS PASSING THROUGH THE LOBBIES AT
9:00 A.M. AND 5:00 P.M.

92-93
THE FALL BRINGS NEW YORK BOTH BRIGHT
AND CLOUDY SKIES, AND THE CITY'S
SKYLINES AND THEIR DETAIL CHANGE
WITH THE LIGHT. VISITORS LOVE CLEAR,
BRILLIANT DAYS THAT HIGHLIGHT BATTERY
PARK CITY, THE TWIN TOWERS AND THE
WATERSIDE BUILDINGS OF THE WORLD
FINANCIAL CENTER.

THE NEW HEART OF THE FINANCIAL DISTRICT

CHAPTER

world tra

WTO

de center

SEPTEMBER 11, 2001

The flamebursts and plumes of smoke are seared into people's memories worldwide. No event in the history became known throughout the world so quickly or so dramatically, or was so symbolic. The Twin Towers rise 1,360 feet in the center of one of the world's most densely populated cities. It's likely that more people saw the flames, the smoke, and the collapse of the shimmering Twin Towers with their own eyes than ever witnessed any other urban disaster.

Within the hour on that warm, sunny morning there was nothing that anyone could say that was new or different: TV commentators left no thought unexpressed. People spoke to comfort each other or to break through the numbness that shock produced rather than to make any informative statement. The suddenness, the enormity and the totality of the event was overwhelming; it is impossible to comprehend such virulent hate, such murderous intent.

The multiple-thrust response to the attack showed near-miraculous efficiency and focus. The speed of action, the scale of operations, and the courage of all who participated make for a memorable chapter in the nation's history.

Heroism was the characteristic of the day. A woman in a wheel chair is carried down endless flights of stairs, a blind man and his dog are escorted down, people assist the injured and disabled. Executives making a last check that all employees are safely out leave too late to save themselves. Some twenty senior World Trade Center staff perish on site, ensuring others will survive. The Fire Department's chaplain, giving the Last Rites to dying firemen, becomes a victim. The courage that kept firemen, police officers, and other rescue personnel in the danger zone, helping people to escape, cost them their lives when the towers collapsed.

New York's Emergency Command Center—in the WTC—was totally destroyed; nonetheless, emergency plans clicked in instantly. Within minutes, disciplined teams of rescue personnel were doing everything the flame-wracked, smoke-billowing site allowed for. Fire engines and ambulances raced down traffic-free avenues; hospitals in Manhattan and neighboring New Jersey moved into emergency operating mode—for all too few survivors.

In Greenwich Village, a mile and a half north of the WTC, people flooded onto the streets within minutes of the first attack. Most witnessed the collapse of the South Tower at 9:50 a.m., while the North Tower, still billowing flame and smoke, collapsed at 10:29. Horrified watchers saw people jumping from high floors, tiny colored dots within the flumes of falling débris. A sense of the unreal—the surreal—pervaded; people looked into the eyes of complete strangers, uncomprehending. Many clasped each other; some sat on the curbs; some sobbed, knowing that people they loved were dying or must have died in horrific circumstances. The Village cafés had their TV sets locked to the news channel; people watch blankly, unable to speak.

Everything known was instantly broadcast, but little new information was forthcoming. No one would (or perhaps could) estimate the death toll. It was a morning of endless streams of people shambling north up the Avenue of the Americas. Most were in shock, many layered in ash and soot, holding onto companions while local residents desperately dialed on cell-phones, trying to put victims in touch with their families. Here and there exhausted people sat on the sidewalks. Farther south, nearer to Ground Zero, it was worse, with people crowding into building lobbies, bleeding, hysterical or traumatized into silence. In the Village cafés, waitresses gently handed out coffee to those who stumbled in, most dazed though unscratched; the visibly injured or disabled had been picked up farther south. All day long the sirens wailed as emergency vehicles sped south; all day long ambulances raced up the Avenue of the Americas toward St. Vincent's Medical Center. There people were parked all along the hospital forecourt in wheel-chairs— mainly in shock. A huge command post sprang up with well over fifty emergency workers and a hundred volunteers.

The city rapidly went into high alert status, with bridges and tunnels closed and subway and train service suspended. Despite the horrific shock and massive dislocation the attack caused, the call was for the maintenance of order: stay calm, cope with

102
THE EMPIRE STATE BUILDING, SOME 50
BLOCKS NORTH OF THE DEVASTATED
WORLD TRADE CENTER AREA, REMAINS A
FAMILIAR AND COMFORTING PRESENCE.

FROM PAGE 103 TO PAGE 107
AT 9:03, THE SECOND BOEING 767 HIT
THE SOUTH TOWER; THE 767'S 20,000
GALLONS OF JET FUEL IGNITED, CREATING A
BLAZING INFERNO.

FROM PAGE 108 TO PAGE 111
THE SOUTH TOWER, THE SECOND TO BE
HIT, WAS THE FIRST TO COLLAPSE
(9:50 A.M.), CONDEMNING THOUSANDS
TRAPPED WITHIN TO A HORRIFIC DEATH.

transportation problems, Move on . . . New York is functioning—shaken but NOT destroyed! The broad artery of Fourteenth Street, running east-west clean across Manhattan, became a manned boundary. To the north, as much normality as possible; to the south, the avenues and streets open to pedestrians only. Further south, Houston (or "First") Street, another major east-west artery, marked a tightly controlled no-access zone; below it, emergency crews and supplies were assembling.

By 6:00 p.m. the patient inflow to the hospitals had diminished to a trickle; no more survivors could be found. The whole WTC area was one vast mound of smoking rubble, hundreds of feet high, spilling over into adjacent streets. The news coverage was of course constant—terrible figures flowing out; 78 police officers unaccounted for, 200 firemen unaccounted for. Some 50,000 people work at the WTC; some 20,000 more are in the area on business visits. Those killed would be numbered in the thousands.

By mid-evening limited subway service was operating and outbound bridge and tunnel crossings were restored in an effort to clear Manhattan of non-residents and non-essential outsiders. New Yorkers recognized that effective management was in place and emergency

operations were going according to plan. The street crowds thinned around 8.30 p.m. as people went home to listen to President Bush address the nation. A judicious speech with only the hint of possible military retaliation. But how does a nation retaliate against an enemy whose weapons are furtiveness and stealth, the murder of the innocent, an enemy too cowardly to ever take the field or stand in the light of day? After the president's address, people again took to the streets, restlessly wandering from St. Vincent's down to the Houston Street barriers and back.

Toward midnight a major quasi-military operation became apparent. Convoys of dump-trucks, bulldozers, plank-and-scaffold trucks parked along Houston Street. At intervals they would roll on down the Avenue of the Americas toward the still burning WTC area. The local fire-station became a command post; for a brief time earlier in the day, before more suitable space could be found closer to the WTC, it had been Mayor Giuliani's Command HQ. The local baseball court became a supply depot; nearby the Salvation Army set up mobile canteens.

To the north, St. Vincent's Medical Center was fully established as a major receiving station, the avenue lit up with floodlights and awash with local residents, the media, and would-be

volunteers. These were in excess of need; by noon it had become was clear that there would be few survivors, only a massive hetacomb of entombed dead. Emergency morgues were being set up locally and across the river in New Jersey. Thousands who had not escaped would be burned, or crushed or mangled beyond recognition—with the terrible result that many families would have no closure, no solace of burying their lost. A gruesome task lay ahead: removing the fragmentary remains of what might at first estimates amount to 10,000 bodies.

A month later New Yorkers were going about their business and living their lives. Everywhere, except at Ground Zero and the immediate area, there is at first glance the appearance of normality. It's the second glance that notes the uniformed security guard, the screening device, the cautionary notice. It's those who have taken an airline flight or had business in a government building that know life is not the same. The news is no longer about other countries and other people. At the core, it is about the United States and the challenge it faces. Violence is a threat; vulnerability is a fact of life. The hope must be that justice and sanity prevail. *(Events as viewed from Greenwich Village, NYC).*

FROM PAGE 128 TO PAGE 133
NEW YORK FIRE DEPARTMENT HAS
WRITTEN A TRAGIC AND UNFORGETTABLE
CHAPTER IN THE CITY'S HISTORY.
THE LOSSES: NEW YORK FIRE
DEPARTMENT AND EMERGENCY MEDICAL
SERVICES, 343; PORT AUTHORITY
(WTC MANAGEMENT), 74; NEW YORK
POLICE DEPARTMENT, 23 LIVES.

134 AND 134-135
ALMOST EVERY NYFD MEMBER LOST
TRUSTED FIREFIGHTER COLLEAGUES; SOME
UNITS HAD ONLY A HANDFUL OF
SURVIVORS. BOTTOM: THE FIRE
DEPARTMENT'S CHAPLAIN, FATHER MYCHAL
JUDGE, WAS AMONG THE HEROES
WHO LOST THEIR LIVES IN THE LINE
OF DUTY.

136 TOP AND 137 TOP
SEVERE EXTERNAL AND INTERNAL DAMAGE
AT THE WORLD FINANCIAL CENTER,
ADJOINING THE WORLD TRADE CENTER.

136-137
BURNED DOCUMENTS SYMBOLIZE THE
DISASTER. THE BRONZE "MAN WITH
BRIEFCASE" SYMBOLIZES SURVIVAL AND
FAITH IN THE FUTURE.

138
DANGER, DUST, EXHAUSTION—WITH NO
END IN SIGHT.

139
FOR AMERICANS AND THE WORLD, THE
STARS AND STRIPES ACQUIRED A TRAGIC
NEW ROLE.

SEPTEMBER 11, 2001

world tra

CTC

WT

THE CHALLENGE
OF THE FUTURE

The world shared the grief of the bereaved. In London, Queen Elizabeth II attended the service of mourning in St. Paul's Cathedral; in many European cities, crowds gathered silently in the great squares, carrying candles and American flags. Public figures and private citizens brought flowers, proclamations, and messages of condolence to American embassies and consulates worldwide. In mourning, Americans were moved to act: hundreds of communities donated supplies from food to fire-trucks, thousands of specialists volunteered services and skills, millions of citizens gave to financial relief funds. The nation and the world have affirmed that evil cannot conquer.

New York City's fire and police departments, Port Authority personnel, and WTC-area employees continued to serve, experiencing unquantifiable degrees of emotional stress. The arbitrariness of fate; the lack of closure; the helplessness that fire, darkness and shattered communications had imposed; the debt owed to colleagues who had lost their lives; the challenge of the future—all posed burdens. Though assistive services were readily available, recognition of need troubled many of the previously self-sufficient.

Throughout the world, television brought 9/11 directly into children's consciousness. In response, thousands of school children, living in nations at peace or war-torn, created pictures, poems and prayers. Many were exhibited in New York; their power and poignancy struck every viewer; in many they rekindled the innocence of hope. These children's artworks constitute an archive in the making.

No school in the WTC area sustained direct major damage on 9/11, though students safely evacuated from the two closest witnessed the horror and chaos of the attack. It is premature to speak definitively of long-term psychological damage to children and parents, but that risk has received a full measure of recognition and response.

As a nation, America has taken strength from the willing support of numerous allies, including those among newer national states. Political leaders have visited Washington, D.C. to confirm support or have spoken unequivocally in national legislatures. It is clear that the imperatives of the campaign against terrorism override political differences among states and can bring together nations of different faiths.

The total cost of 9/11 cannot be easily calculated. Replacement costs for physical structures are roughly calculable but business and tax losses, lost jobs, reduced tourism, increased security costs, and the tragic loss of skilled business leaders and employees are not easily calculated. Add to this the previous business slowdown and a nascent recovery, economic activity to be generated by rebuilding operations, future business activity and tourism, and it's clear that talk of $100 billion, with a 20 percent swing factor, is little more than inspired guessing. The federal government's aid package totals $21.5 billion, with $2.75 billion of it for WTC site and area clean-up, and $1.8 billion for subway system repair. Capital costs for a rebuilt transportation hub alone top $7 billion—but in part would fund expanded facilities. Only after below-surface infrastructure is completed can new buildings arise, their costs yet unknown.

At best, redevelopment of the WTC site will prove to be a catalyst for greatly increased economic activity throughout Lower Manhattan. Paradoxically, the greatest long-term costs may accrue to non-allied nations for whom agricultural, industrial, transportation, communications and scientific technologies (the tools of 21st-century progress) are transfers from the West, paid for in oil—whose value decreases as additional oil-producing regions enter the market.

THE CHALLENGE OF THE FUTURE

154 AND 155
"TRIBUTE IN LIGHT" DRAMATICALLY
COMMEMORATED THE SIX-MONTH
ANNIVERSARY OF 9/11. FOR MILLIONS IT
ALSO SIGNALED CONFIDENCE IN NEW YORK
AND ITS FUTURE.

SEPTEMBER 11 MATRIX

HEROES LINES
TO GROUND ZERO

REBUILDING
THE WORLD TRADE CENTER

The "Memory Foundations" project by Studio Daniel Libeskind was chosen by the Lower Manhattan Development Corporation (LMDC) in February of 2003, to give a new form to the World Trade Center site. The fulcrum of the project is One World Trade Center (Tower 1), though the site is also referred to as the Freedom Tower—extending over an area of about 16 acre (6.5 ha). Designed by Skidmore, Owings & Merrill LLP (SOM), One World Trade Center is a tapering building with a height of 1,776 feet (541.32 m), a symbolic number recalling the year of the Declaration of Independence, a momentous date in the history of the United States. Besides the spectacular tower, the project foresees creation of an articulated complex of several structures. At Ground Zero in Lower Manhattan, around the principal skyscraper, other imposing edifices will be rising: the World Trade Center PATH Transportation Hub (or "Transit Hub") planned by Santiago Calatrava, three office towers wrapping spiral-like around One World Trade Center (bearing the names of Two, Three, and Four World Trade Center), a majestic memorial all played upon water basins and waterfalls (whose name, Reflecting Absence, denotes the spirit of the project), an underground museum, a performing arts center, a visitors' center, commercial spaces, and possibly an Islamic cultural center.

In order to realize this project, which will give a new face to the Manhattan skyline, Studio Daniel Libeskind has been coordinating for years the work of the various agencies and enterprises involved:

from the commissioners—principal among whom are the Port Authority of New York and New Jersey, the Lower Manhattan Development Corporation, and Silverstein Properties, Inc.—to the various architectural studios, including: Skidmore, Owings & Merrill LLP (SOM) (One World Trade Center); Foster + Partners (Two World Trade Center); Rogers Stirk Harbour + Partners (Three World Trade Center); Maki and Associates (Four World Trade Center); Santiago Calatrava (Transportation Hub); Michael Arad and Peter Walker (Reflecting Absence); Snøhetta (Visitor Orientation and Education Center); and Davis Brody Bond Aedas (Memorial Museum).

Construction of One World Trade Center commenced in April of 2006. The project was first commissioned by Silverstein Properties Inc., which was later succeeded by the Port Authority. The architect of the project is David Childs of Skidmore, Owings & Merrill LLP. With its 102 stories and its mind-boggling 400-foot (120 m) antenna, One World Trade Center will become the tallest skyscraper in the United States, reaffirming Manhattan's preeminence as a business center and becoming a new symbol of the nation's civic pride. The building will emanate a crystalline quality, will capture and reflect light: depending on the atmospheric conditions and the various hours of the day, the building's surface will take on different appearances, just like a kaleidoscope. The project will make use of security systems and eco-sustainable technologies—such as fire safety

and air filtering—that are absolutely avant-garde.

Work on Two World Trade Center (also known as Tower 2 or 200 Greenwich Street) started in summer of 2008 and is coordinated by Foster + Partners and commissioned by Silverstein Properties Inc. At 79 stories (besides the 2 underground floors), this office tower will have a diamond-like appearance in common with One World Trade Center not only in terms of form, but also in terms of cleanness of surface. The building will rise at the northeast corner of Memorial Park. Two World Trade Center will also employ sophisticated techniques of sustainable architecture and will be the area's second-highest skyscraper, at more than 1,270 feet (387 m) not counting its antenna, which is another 79 feet (24 m) high.

Work on the third-highest building, Three World Trade Center (Tower 3, or 175 Greenwich Street), started in spring of 2008, and was also commissioned by Silverstein Properties Inc. Planned by Richard Rogers of Rogers Stirk Harbour + Partners, the 71-story tower (plus its four floors below street level) will ascend 1,155 feet (352 m) right from the center of the buildings surrounding the memorial, on a lot delimited by Greenwich Street to the west, Church Street to the east, Dey Street to the north, and Cortlandt Street to the south.

The area's fourth highest skyscraper, Four World Trade Center (Tower 4 or 150 Greenwich Street), designed by Fumihiko Maki of Maki and Associates, will rise to 947 feet (289 m) from the area between Greenwich, Liberty, Church, and

Cortlandt Streets, for a total of 61 stories over street level.

The four towers as a complex will restore the spirit of a place that in recent decades has been the heart of an active community. Each tower will reflect the individual genius of the architect who designed it, but at the same time, will integrate in perfect harmony with the others. These buildings will be joined by other nearby structures, such as the new Seven World Trade Center, also a work by David Childs of SOM, and situated at 250 Greenwich Street. This 52-story tower, simple and functional in form, was completed in 2006 and, joined by other new projects, is a symbol of rebirth for the Downtown Manhattan area.

Work began in 2006 for construction of the National September 11 Memorial & Museum. It will include a museum (planned by Davis Brody Bond and Snøhetta) and Reflecting Absence, the memorial work by Michael Arad and landscape architect Peter Walker. The memorial is formed by two square basins situated at the exact sites from which the Twin Towers rose, surrounded by the September 11 Plaza, which is planted with oak trees. Water will flow in cascades into each of the two basins, which will be illuminated. The names of the 2,979 victims of the attacks of September 11, 2001 will be inscribed around the edges of the pools.

To complete the work, the museum, planned by Davis Brody Bond will provide more profound contact with the place; visitors will access the museum through an entrance pavilion designed by Snøhetta. Gehry Partners LLP was entrusted with realization of the Performing Arts Center, which will rise beside One World Trade Center at the corner between Fulton Street and Greenwich Street, with seats for some 1,000 spectators.

Santiago Calatrava conceived the Transportation Hub to substitute the old World Trade Center Station: with its graceful, undulating lines, the station will provide not only access to the World Trade Center area, but an auspice of beauty and reawakening for an area so brutally put to test.

158

THIS DRAWING, PRESENTED BY STUDIO DANIEL LIBESKIND TO THE ARCHITECTURAL COMPETITION FOR RECONSTRUCTION OF THE GROUND ZERO AREA ALREADY SHOWS THE SPIRAL OF SKYSCRAPERS THAT DEVELOPS AROUND THE BROAD CENTRAL SPACE WITHIN THE MEMORIAL. TO THE LEFT, ONE TOWER STANDS HIGHER THAN ALL THE OTHERS, ONE WORLD TRADE CENTER (TOWER 1), LATER CONCEIVED BY SOM.

159

AFTER APPROVAL OF THE PRELIMINARY PLAN BY LIBESKIND, THE PROJECT FOR ONE WORLD TRADE CENTER WAS RE-ELABORATED AND ENTRUSTED TO STUDIO SKIDMORE, OWINGS & MERRILL LLP (SOM). THE SKYSCRAPER WILL OCCUPY THE NORTHWEST CORNER OF THE SITE WHERE ONCE THE WORLD TRADE CENTER TOWERS ROSE, BETWEEN VESEY STREET, WEST STREET (ROUTE 9A), WASHINGTON STREET, AND FULTON STREET.

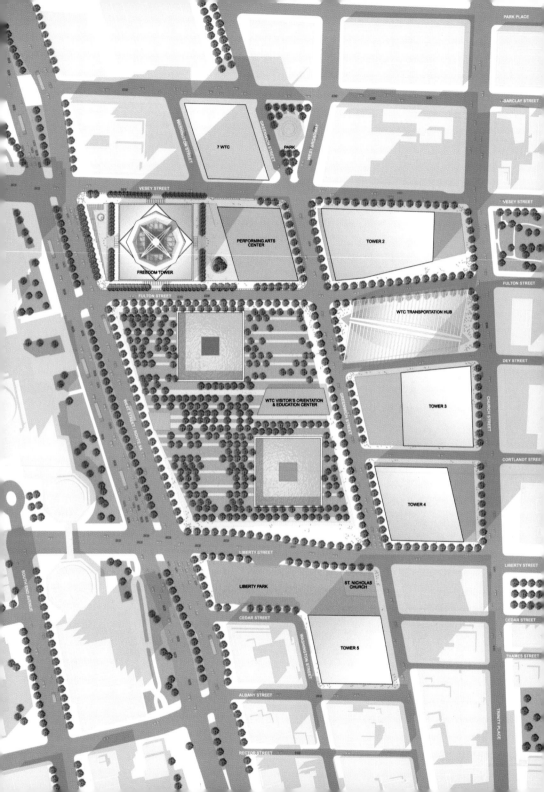

160-161

THE DEFINITIVE PROJECT FOR
RECONSTRUCTION OF THE AREA, PRESENTED
IN JUNE OF 2006, WILL PRODUCE AN EFFECT
SIMILAR TO THAT DEPICTED IN THIS
RENDERING. THE MANHATTAN SKYLINE WILL
BE DOMINATED BY ONE WORLD TRADE
CENTER: IT WILL TOWER ABOVE ALL THE
SURROUNDING BUILDINGS WITH ITS HEIGHT
OF 1,776 FEET (541.32 M), A FIGURE THAT
ALLUDES TO THE YEAR OF THE DECLARATION
OF INDEPENDENCE.

162
THE REBIRTH OF LOWER MANHATTAN, AFTER
THE GREATEST TRAGEDY IN THE HISTORY OF NEW
YORK AND OF THE ENTIRE NATION, TESTIFIES
TO THE COURAGE OF NEW YORKERS, TO THEIR
CREATIVITY, AND TO THEIR DETERMINATION TO
RECONSTRUCT A PART OF THE CITY TO A LEVEL
EVEN BETTER THAN BEFORE, CREATING NEW
AND MEANINGFUL RELATIONSHIPS BETWEEN
THE INDIVIDUAL BUILDINGS AND THE
SURROUNDING URBAN FABRIC.

163
THE RENDERING OF THE PROJECT
CURRENTLY UNDERWAY SHOWS HOW
THE FOUR PRINCIPAL TOWERS—AS
FORESEEN BY LIBESKIND IN HIS CONCEPTION
OF THE MASTER PLAN—GO TO FORM
A SORT OF SPIRAL DESCENDING TOWARD
THE MEMORIAL AND SEPTEMBER 11 PLAZA,
EMBRACED BETWEEN FULTON STREET
TO THE NORTH AND LIBERTY STREET
TO THE SOUTH.

164

IN THIS RENDERING DEPICTING THE FUTURE
SKYLINE OF LOWER MANHATTAN, THE
STATUE OF LIBERTY, THE ICONIC SYMBOL
OF NEW YORK AND OF THE UNITED STATES,
APPEARS TO HOLD VIGIL OVER THE CITY WHILE
AWAITING FINAL COMPLETION OF THIS
MIRACULOUS AND DIFFICULT RECONSTRUCTION.

164-165

THE NEW WORLD TRADE CENTER BUILDINGS—
AND IN PARTICULAR, TWO, THREE AND FOUR
WORLD TRADE CENTER, WHICH FACE ONTO
GREENWICH STREET (AT CENTER)—COULD
SERVE AS PARADIGMS FOR THE MODERN
SKYSCRAPER IN TERMS OF ECO-SUSTAINABILITY,
ENERGY SAVINGS, QUALITY OF LIFE, AND SAFETY.

GROUND FLOOR PLAN

VESEY STREET

WEST STREET

FULTON STREET

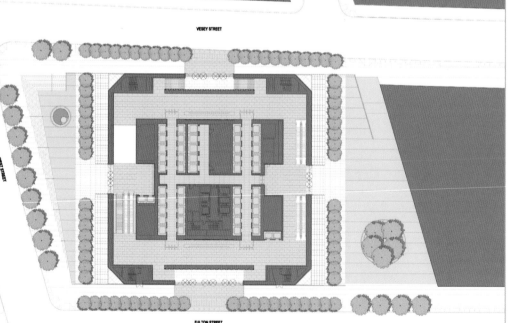

166 TOP
ONE WORLD TRADE CENTER STANDS
OUT FOR CLEANNESS OF FORM AND
DOES NOT APPEAR DESTINED FOR
A PRECOCIOUS OBSOLESCENCE.

166 BOTTOM
THE TOWER RISES FROM A CUBIC BASEMENT.
AT ITS MIDDLE, THE SQUARE OF THE BASE
TRANSFORMS INTO A PERFECT OCTAGON,
CULMINATING THEN AT THE SUMMIT
IN A GLASS PARAPET OF SQUARE FORM,
BUT ROTATED 45° FROM THE BASE.

167
WHEREAS THE MEMORIAL BELOW, DUG
LITERALLY INTO THE GROUND, SPEAKS TO
US OF THE PAST AND OF MEMORIES,
ONE WORLD TRADE CENTER IS A SYMBOL
OF HOPE FOR THE FUTURE, EVOKING, WITH
ITS SLENDER, TAPERING FORM, SOME OF
THE TIMELESS ICONS OF NEW YORK CITY,
SUCH AS THE CHRYSLER BUILDING AND
THE EMPIRE STATE BUILDING.

167

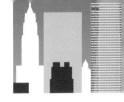

168 TOP LEFT
THE LARGE, LUMINOUS LOBBY FORMS
THE CENTRAL NUCLEUS OF THE TOWER,
FLOODED BY NATURAL LIGHT COMING
THROUGH ENTRANCES SITUATED
TO THE EAST AND WEST, AS WELL AS
BY OPENINGS AT THE NORTH AND
SOUTH SIDES OF THE BUILDING.

168 TOP RIGHT
THE IMAGE DEPICTS A SECTIONAL VIEW OF
THE CURTAIN WALL: WORKING IN CLOSE
CONTACT WITH INDUSTRY EXPERTS, THE
PROJECT PLANNERS STUDIED THESE GLASS

WALLS, AND TOGETHER THEY SUCCEEDED IN
DEVELOPING A NEW TYPE OF PANEL CAPABLE
OF RESISTING HIGH WINDSAND EXPLOITING
NATURAL LIGHT, AS WELL AS CONFERRING
AN IMPRESSION OF SOLEMN MONUMENTALITY
UPON THE TOWER.

168-169
AT THE BASE OF THE BUILDING, THE
PLANNERS' EFFORT WAS TO CREATE AN AIRY
STRUCTURE, WHICH WOULD OPEN ONTO
EXTERIOR PLAZAS WHERE PEOPLE CAN
MEET, SIT, RELAX, AND STOP TO THINK.
THE RENDERING SHOWS THE WEST PLAZA.

171 TOP
THE RENDERING DEPICTS THE GROUND
FLOOR PLAN FOR TWO WORLD TRADE
CENTER DESIGNED BY FOSTER + PARTNERS.

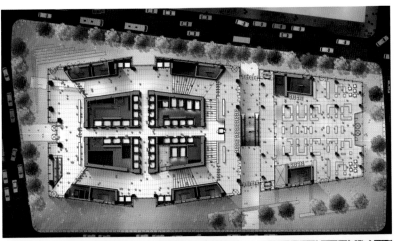

170
THE TRUNK OF TWO WORLD TRADE
CENTER (TOWER 2) IS ARTICULATED
INTO FOUR INTERCONNECTED BLOCKS.
AT THE 64TH STORY IT IS CUT DIAGONALLY,
RECALLING THE FORM OF THE MEMORIAL.

171 CENTER
THE TOWER DEVELOPS AROUND
A CROSS-SHAPED CENTRAL NUCLEUS.
THE LOBBY IS TRIPLE HEIGHT AND
ALLOWS DIRECT ACCESS TO THE SUBWAY.

171 BOTTOM
AT STREET LEVEL, THE BUILDING'S
RELATIONSHIP WITH THE CITY FABRIC
IS REFLECTED IN WALLS OF GLASS, AND
CREATES A VISUAL RAPPORT BETWEEN THE
INTERIOR AND THE SURROUNDING STREETS.

172
In the external bearing structure of Three World Trade Center (Tower 3), diagonal elements played around a base module of 16 floors stand out, and emphasize the tower's verticality.

173 TOP
The rendering of the lobby at Three World Trade Center displays an airy and luminous environment that will serve as the entrance to the building as well as a connection to the subway and commercial spaces.

173 BOTTOM
The project accentuates the centrality of the skyscraper within the area, and at the same time emphasizes its verticality in relation to the memorial site.

THE CHALLENGE OF THE FUTURE

174
ALONG WITH TOWER 2 AND TOWER 3,
FOUR WORLD TRADE CENTER (TOWER 4)
WILL BE SITUATED ALONG THE EAST MARGIN
OF THE WORLD TRADE CENTER SITE.
THE PROJECT APPROACH IS, ON THE ONE
HAND, "MINIMALIST": MAKI WANTED
TO MAKE THE TOWER A TRANQUIL BUT
DIGNIFIED PRESENCE, SUITED TO THE PLACE
AND CIRCUMSTANCE; ON THE OTHER HAND,
HE AIMED AT CONFERRING UPON IT A
POWERFUL PRESENCE, TO BE UTTERLY
RECOGNIZABLE WITHIN THE MANHATTAN
SKYLINE, EVEN AT A DISTANCE, OWING
TO ITS ANGULAR PROFILE.

175 CENTER AND BOTTOM
THE BASEMENT, WITH ITS "MATERIALITY,"
PLAYS UPON THE RELATIONSHIP BETWEEN GLASS
AND METAL, AND WAS CONCEIVED TO ENLIVEN
THE SURROUNDING URBAN AREA.

THE CHALLENGE OF THE FUTURE

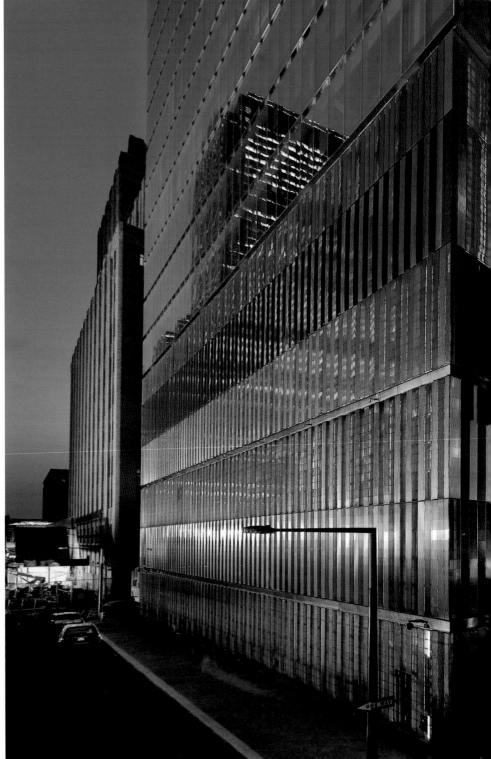

178

THE NEW MASTER PLAN HAS RADICALLY MODIFIED THE CONTEXT IN WHICH THE REBORN SEVEN WORLD TRADE CENTER DEVELOPED: THE ORIGINAL STRUCTURE COULD BE ACCESSED ONLY THROUGH THE PODIUM, FOUR STORIES ABOVE THE STREET LEVEL, WHEREAS THIS NEW PROJECT RESPONDS TO MORE COMPLEX REQUIREMENTS FOR COMMUNICATION AMONG THE PUBLIC SPACES.

178-179

THE NEW TOWER—THE RENDERING HERE DEPICTS THE BASEMENT—WAS CONCEIVED AS A GREAT MULTI-FACET CRYSTAL FROM WHICH LIGHT APPEARS TO EMANATE SPONTANEOUSLY, SPREADING OUTWARD. THE RESULT IS THAT THE BUILDING PRACTICALLY MELDS TOGETHER WITH THE SKY, GLITTERING MAGICALLY, ESPECIALLY BY NIGHT.

180-181 TOP
REFLECTING ABSENCE, THE PROJECT BY
MICHAEL ARAD AND PETER WALKER FOR
SEPTEMBER 11 PLAZA, CALLS FOR CREATING
A VAST TREE-LINED PLAZA IN WHICH TWO
ENORMOUS EMPTY SPACES FILLED WITH WATER
WILL RECALL THE SITES FROM WHICH THE
TWIN TOWERS ROSE. THE BASINS WILL
BE FED BY CONTINUOUS CASCADES OF WATER
AND WILL BEAR THE ENGRAVED NAMES
OF THE VICTIMS OF THE ATTACKS.

180-181 BOTTOM
THE MEMORIAL MUSEUM, DESIGNED
BY DAVIS BRODY BOND TO BE BUILT
BENEATH THE PLAZA, WILL NARRATE THE
HEARTBREAKING AND HEROIC EVENTS OF
SEPTEMBER 11. ON THE SURFACE, THE
VISITOR ORIENTATION AND EDUCATION
CENTER, DESIGNED BY NORWEGIAN STUDIO
SNØHETTA, WILL CONSTITUTE ONE OF
THE ENTRIES TO THE UNDERLYING
COMMEMORATIVE SPACES, ALSO
ACCESSIBLE BY RAMPS SITUATED
AROUND THE TWO BASINS.

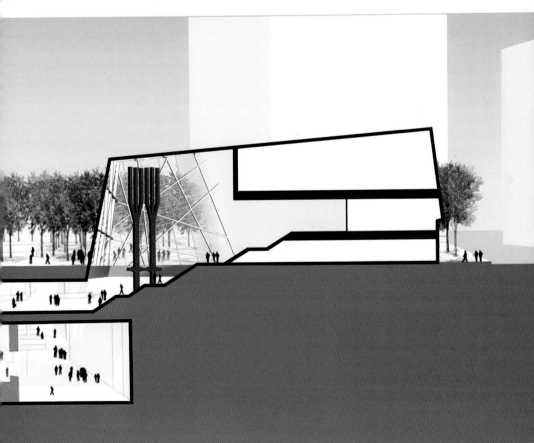

182-183

THE RENDERING SHOWS MORE DETAILED
CHARACTERISTICS OF THE REFLECTING
ABSENCE PROJECT BY ISRAELI ARCHITECT
MICHAEL ARAD, THE FULCRUM OF THE
MEMORIAL TO THE VICTIMS OF THE TERRORIST
ATTACKS. THE TWO BASINS ARE EACH
SITUATED AT A DEPTH OF ABOUT 4 M
(13 FEET) WITH RESPECT TO STREET LEVEL
AND ARE FED BY CONTINUOUS WATER FLOWS,
CREATING A CASCADE EFFECT, A SORT OF
IMPALPABLE VEIL. THE ACCOMPANYING
SOUND OF WATER PRACTICALLY ISOLATES
THE VISITOR FROM THE EXTERNAL WORLD
AND FROM THE NOISES OF THE CITY.

183 BOTTOM

THE TWO GREAT EMPTY SPACES RECALL
TO MEMORY—OR BETTER "REFLECT"—THE
ABSENCE OF THOSE WHO PERISHED ON
SEPTEMBER 11, EVOKING A SENSE OF
IRRETRIEVABLE LOSS, WHICH THE TWO
BASINS OUGHT, IN SOME MANNER, HELP
TO "CONTAIN." THE NAMES OF THE
VICTIMS WILL BE ENGRAVED ON AN ENDLESS
RIBBON THAT WILL RUN ALONG THE
PARAPETS ENCIRCLING THE BASINS.
ACCORDING TO ARAD HIMSELF, THE
PROJECT AIMS AT MAKING VISIBLE
THAT WHICH IS ABSENT, THOSE WE
LOST FOREVER ON THAT TRAGIC DAY.

IN MEMORIAM

184-185

A FUNDAMENTAL AND CHARACTERISTIC ELEMENT OF THE ENTRY PAVILION TO THE MEMORIAL MUSEUM DESIGNED BY SNØHETTA IS THE LARGE ATRIUM NEAR THE CENTER OF THE PLAZA, ALLOWING VISITORS TO SEE THE INTERIOR OF THE MUSEUM, WHERE CERTAIN ARCHITECTURAL COMPONENTS THAT SURVIVED THE COLLAPSE OF THE TWIN TOWERS WILL BE EXHIBITED. THE IMPOSING STEEL COLUMNS VISIBLE AT THE CENTER, ORIGINAL STRUCTURAL ELEMENTS RECOVERED FROM THE TWIN TOWER SITE, ARE CALLED "TRIDENTS" FOR THEIR PARTICULAR FORM, AND CREATE A HARMONIOUS LINK WITH THE OAKS PROLIFERATING ABOUT THE PLAZA.

185

THIS RENDERING DEPICTS SOME OF THE PROPOSALS FOR DISPLAYS OF REMAINS DISCOVERED AT THE SITE OVER WHICH THE TOWERS ROSE, NOT ONLY FOR RECOUNTING THOSE TERRIBLE EVENTS OF 9/11, BUT ALSO TO TESTIFY TO ALL THE ALTRUISM, DEDICATION, AND COMPASSION—AT TIMES TO THE POINT OF SACRIFICE OF LIFE ITSELF—ON THAT SAD DAY AND, FURTHER STILL, IN THE FOLLOWING WEEKS AND MONTHS. THESE STORIES WILL BE RELATED THROUGH THE OBJECTS ON DISPLAY AND BY MEANS OF MULTIMEDIA PRESENTATIONS.

186-187

A SECTION OF THE FOUNDATION WALL FOR
THE WORLD TRADE CENTER, THE SLURRY
WALL, WILL BE EXHIBITED AT THE HEART
OF THE ENORMOUS WEST CHAMBER OF
THE UNDERGROUND MUSEUM, WHERE AN
IMPOSING COLUMN THAT SURVIVED THE
COLLAPSE OF THE TOWERS WILL ALSO BE SEEN.

188-189
SANTIAGO CALATRAVA IS RESPONSIBLE FOR THE
FUTURISTIC BUILDING OF THE WORLD TRADE
CENTER PATH TRANSPORTATION HUB,
WITH ITS INCREDIBLY SLENDER SILHOUETTE.
LIGHT COMING THROUGH THE GLASS ROOF
WILL ILLUMINATE THE GREAT INTERIOR SPACE.

189 BOTTOM
THE "TRANSIT HUB" WILL RISE FROM THE
NORTHEAST CORNER OF THE SITE AND WILL
BE CONNECTED TO FULTON STREET TRANSIT
CENTER VIA UNDERGROUND PASSAGEWAYS
TO THE WORLD FINANCIAL CENTER.

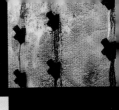

190-191
FOR MANY NEW YORKERS, THE MOST
SIGNIFICANT ASPECT OF THIS HARMONIOUS
NEW URBAN ENVIRONMENT AND WELL
PROPORTIONED SKYLINE WILL BE THAT
THEIR BELOVED CITY CONTINUES TO LIVE
AND THRIVE, EVEN AS IT STILL WORKS
TO OVERCOME THE PAIN AND LOSS
OF SEPTEMBER 11, 2001.

PHOTO CREDITS

Page 1: Marcello Bertinetti/Archivio White Star
Pages 2-3: Space Imaging
Pages 4-5: Antonio Attini/Archivio White Star
Pages 6-7: Cesare Gerolimetto/Archivio White Star
Page 8 left: Roger et Voillet/Contrasto
Page 9 left: Everett Collection/Granata Press Service
Page 9 center: Glamour International/Agefotostock/Contrasto
Page 9 right: Robert Clark/Aurora/Grazia Neri
Page 10: Joseph Pobereskin/Agefotostock/Contrasto
Page 11 top: Leroy/Saba/Contrasto
Page 12 bottom: Maiselas/Magnum/Contrasto
Pages 12-13: Antonio Attini/Archivio White Star
Pages 14-15: Allan Tannenbaum/Gamma/Contrasto
Page 16 top: M. Gratton/Vision
Page 17: Agefotostock/Contrasto
Page 18: Naomi Stock/Time Pix/Photo Masi
Page 19 bottom: Gamma/Contrasto
Pages 20-21: Marcello Bertinetti/Archivio White Star
Pages 22-23: Chris Corder/Gamma/Contrasto
Page 26 top: Library of Congress
Page 27: Photos12
Pages 28-29: Photos12
Page 29: Luke Bennett/New York Stock Photo
Page 30 top: Roger et Voillet/Contrasto
Pages 30-31: Photos12
Page 31 bottom: Cornell Capa/Magnum/Contrasto
Page 32 top: Roger et Voillet/Contrasto
Page 32 center: Hulton Archive/Laura Ronchi
Pages 32-33: Roger et Voillet/Contrasto
Pages 34-35: Hulton Archive/Laura Ronchi
Page 39: Joseph Rosen/New York Stock Photo
Pages 40-41: Balthazar Korab Photography
Page 42 top left and right: Balthazar Korab Photography
Page 43 top: Balthazar Korab Photography
Pages 44, 45: Balthazar Korab Photography
Page 46 top: Balthazar Korab Photography
Page 47: Balthazar Korab Photography
Pages 48-49: Philipe I. Beane/Mary Evans Picture Library
Page 51: Douglas Dickins/Mary Evans Picture library
Page 52: Douglas Dickins/Mary Evans Picture Library
Page 53 top: Douglas Dickins/Mary Evans Picture Library
Page 53 bottom: Jeffrey J. Foxx/Woodfin Camp Associates
Pages 54-55: Archivio Domus/Editoriale Domus
Page 55 top: Archivio Domus/Editoriale Domus
Page 56: Marcello Bertinetti/Archivio White Star
Page 57 top: Balthazar Korab Photography
Page 57 center left: Ettagale Laure/ Woodfin Camp Associates
Page 57 center right: Marcello Bertinetti/Archivio White Star
Page 57 bottom: Marcello Bertinetti/Archivio White Star
Page 59: Marcello Bertinetti/Archivio White Star
Pages 60-61: Lawrence A. Martin/Artifice Inc.
Pages 62-63: NYC Office of Emergency Management/Associated Press
Page 63 top: Esbin Anderson/Agefotostock/Contrasto
Pages 64-65: Space Imaging
Page 65 bottom: Gamma/Contrasto
Page 68 top: Associated Press
Page 69: Associated Press
Pages 70-71: Marvin Newman/Woodfin Camp Associates
Page 71 bottom: Balthazar Korab Photography
Page 72 top: Richard Nowitz/Marka
Pages 72-73: Peter Bennett/New York Stock Photo
Page 73 bottom: Charlyn Zlotnik/Woodfin Camp Associates
Page 74: Marvin Newman/Woodfin Camp Associates
Page 75: Stefano Cellai
Page 76 bottom: Dan Heller Photography
Pages 76-77: Sime Photo
Pages 78, 79: Everett Collection/Granata
Pages 80, 81: Everett Collection/Granata
Page 84 top: Antonio Attini/Archivio White Star

Page 85: Zefa
Page 86 bottom: Antonio Attini/Archivio White Star
Pages 86-87: Zefa
Pages 88-89: Antonio Attini/Archivio White Star
Page 89 bottom: Zefa
Pages 90, 91: Balthazar Korab Photography
Pages 92-93: Sime Photo
Pages 96, 97: Robert Clark/Aurora/Grazia Neri
Pages 98-99: Naomi Stock/Time Pix/Photo Masi
Page 100: Doug Mills/Associated Press
Page 101: Shawn Baldwin/Associated Press
Page 102: Patrick Sison/Associated Press
Page 103 top: Carmen Taylor/Associated Press
Pages 104-105: Mark Stetler/Saba/Contrasto
Pages 106-107: Thierry Tinacci/Saba/Contrasto
Page 108: Amy Sancetta/Associated Press
Page 109 top and bottom: Reuters/Olympia
Pages 110, 111: Richard Drew/Associated Press
Page 112 top: Robert Stolarik/Gamma/Contrasto
Pages 112-113: S. Plunkett/Associated Press
Pages 114-115: Richard Drew/Associated Press
Page 116: D. Surowiecki/Getty Images/LaPresse
Page 117 top: Jonathan De Marco/Gamma/Contrasto
Page 117 bottom: Reuters/Olympia
Pages 118-119: Zuma Press/Red Dot/Mishaishat/Gamma/Contrasto
Page 119: Suzanne Plunket/Associated Press
Pages 120-121: Hoepker/Magnum/Contrasto
Page 122 top: Gilles Peres/Magnum/Contrasto
Pages 122-123: Patrick Andrade/Gamma/Contrasto
Page 123 top: Robert Stolarik/Gamma/Contrasto
Pages 124-125: D. Bondareff/Associated Press
Page 125 top: Robert Stolarik/Gamma/Contrasto
Page 125 right: Gilles Peres/Magnum/Contrasto
Page 126: Gilles Peres/Magnum/Contrasto
Page 127: Meiselas/Magnum Contrasto
Pages 128-129: Saba/Contrasto
Page 129 top: Saba/Contrasto
Pages 130-131: Gilles Peres/Magnum/Contrasto
Pages 132-133: Gilles Peres/Magnum/Contrasto
Page 134 top: Getty Images/LaPresse
Pages 134-135: S. Stapleton/Reuters/Olympia
Page 136 top: Tim Fadek/Gamma/ Contrasto
Pages 136-137: C. Jones/Saba/Contrasto
Page 137 top: Tim Fadek/Gamma/ Contrasto
Page 138: Gamma/Contrasto
Page 139: Franklin/Magnum/Contrasto
Page 140, 141: Eric Tilford/Associated Press
Pages 142-143: Tim Fadek/Gamma/Contrasto
Page 144: Daniele Dainelli/Contrasto
Pages 144-145: Ed Betz/Associated Press
Pages 146-147: Webb/Magnum/Contrasto
Page 150 top: The WTC Children's Mural Project
Page 151: Mark Lennihan/Agency Press
Pages 152-153: Stuart Ramson/Agency Press
Page 154: Catherine Leuthild/Agency Press
Page 155: Ray Stubblebine/Reuters/Publiphoto Olympia
Page 156: courtesy of the Studio Daniel Libeskind
Page 157: courtesy of the Studio Daniel Libeskind
Page 158: Archimation, courtesy of the Studio Daniel Libeskind
Page 159: courtesy of the Skidmore, Owings & Merrill LLP (SOM)
Pages 160-161: courtesy of the Silverstein Properties (SPI)
Page 162: courtesy of the RRP, Team Macarie
Page 163: courtesy of the Silverstein Properties (SPI)
Page 164: courtesy of the Studio Daniel Libeskind
Pages 164-165: courtesy of the Silverstein Properties (SPI)
Page 166 top: courtesy of the Skidmore, Owings & Merrill LLP (SOM)
Page 166 bottom: courtesy of the Skidmore, Owings & Merrill LLP (SOM)
Page 167: courtesy of the Skidmore, Owings & Merrill LLP (SOM)
Page 168: courtesy of the Skidmore, Owings & Merrill LLP (SOM)
Pages 168-169: courtesy of the Skidmore, Owings & Merrill LLP (SOM)
Page 170: courtesy of the Foster + Partners / Silverstein Properties (SPI)
Page 171 top: courtesy of the Foster + Partners/Silverstein Properties (SPI)
Page 171 center: courtesy of the Foster + Partners/Silverstein Properties (SPI)

Page 171 bottom: courtesy of the Foster + Partners/Silverstein Properties (SPI)
Page 172: courtesy of the Rogers Stirk Harbour + Partners
Page 173 top: courtesy of the Rogers Stirk Harbour + Partners
Page 173 bottom: courtesy of the Rogers Stirk Harbour + Partners
Page 174: courtesy of the Maki and Associates
Page 175 top: courtesy of the Maki and Associates
Page 175 bottom: courtesy of the Maki and Associates
Pag 176: courtesy of the Skidmore, Owings & Merrill LLP (SOM)
Pages 176-177: Ruggero Vanni, courtesy of the Skidmore, Owings & Merrill LLP (SOM)
Page 178: courtesy of the Skidmore, Owings & Merrill LLP (SOM)
Pages 178-179: courtesy of the Skidmore, Owings & Merrill LLP (SOM)
Pages 180-181 top: courtesy of the National September 11 Memorial & Museum, rendering by Squared Design Lab
Pages 180-181 bottom: courtesy of the Snøhetta
Pages 182-183: courtesy of the National September 11 Memorial & Museum, rendering by Squared Design Lab
Page 183: courtesy of the National September 11 Memorial & Museum, rendering by Squared Design Lab
Page 184: courtesy of the Snøhetta, rendering by Squared Design Lab
Page 185 top: courtesy of the National September 11 Memorial & Museum/Thinc Design with Local Projects
Page 185 center: courtesy of the National September 11 Memorial & Museum/Thinc Design with Local Projects
Page 185 bottom: courtesy of the National September 11 Memorial & Museum/Thinc Design with Local Projects
Pages 186-187: courtesy of the National September 11 Memorial & Museum, rendering by Squared Design Lab
Pages 188-189, 189: courtesy of the Santiago Calatrava / Studio Daniel Libeskind
Pages 190-191: courtesy of the Silverstein Properties (SPI)

The Publisher would like to thank:

Archivio Editoriale Domus: Carmen Figini
Foster + Partners: Lauren Catten, Gayle Mault and Kathryn Tollervey
Fabio Grazioli
Maki and Associates: Joyce Factor Tan
Minoru Yamasaki Associates
National September 11 Memorial & Museum: Jenna Moonan and Lynn Rasic
PWP Landscape Architecture: Kay Cheng
Rogers Stirk Harbour + Partners: Jenny Stephens
Silverstein Properties (SPI): Dara McQuillan and Rebecca Shalomoff
Skidmore, Owings & Merrill LLP (SOM): Landis Carey and Elizabeth Kubany
Snøhetta: Kira Kupfersberger
Studio Daniel Libeskind: Amanda Ice and Alex Rabe
The New York Times
The Port Authority of New York & New Jersey: Steve Coleman and Frank Pita
The Skyscraper Museum, New York
World Trade Center Association, Rome: Veronica Di Nardo and Piero Piccardi

The author is deeply grateful to Mike Wallace for generous encouragement.

Translation of chapter "The Twin Towers: design and architecture" by CTM, Milan.

The subchapter "Rebuilding the World Trade Center" in the chapter "The Challenge of the Future" was produced by the editing department. Translation by John Venerella.

EDITORIAL COORDINATION:
LAURA ACCOMAZZO, FEDERICA ROMAGNOLI, MARIA VALERIA URBANI GRECCHI, CLAUDIA ZANERA